NO COMPROMISE

THE TRUTH ABOUT WORKPLACE SAFETY & BUSINESS SUCCESS

NO COMPROMISE

THE TRUTH ABOUT **WORKPLACE SAFETY** & **BUSINESS SUCCESS**

KEN SHERIDAN

gatekeeper press™
Columbus, Ohio

NO COMPROMISE

The truth about workplace safety and business success

Published by **Gatekeeper Press**

2167 Stringtown Rd, Suite 109

Columbus, OH 43123-2989

www.GatekeeperPress.com

Edited by **Phyllis G. Gamache**

Library of Congress Control Number: 2022932828

ISBN (paperback): 9781662924385
ISBN (hardcover): 9781662930003
eISBN: 9781662924392

This book is dedicated to every person
in the electrical utility industry in the US and worldwide.
Each of you has my admiration and respect for choosing a trade that asks you to
work under extremely dangerous and in extreme weather conditions.
Your professionalism and commitment to your trade serves millions of customers
who will never know your name but owe you a debt of gratitude.

"This book is as genuine as the man who wrote it. It gives you the key elements you need to improve safety performance within your organisation. No snake oil, no flim flam, just honest and straightforward advice for leaders and safety professionals who want to make the change and make it stick."

—**ANDY MURDY**,
CMIOSH Founder, Explorator Consulting Limited

* * *

"Ken Sheridan has been a safety leader, safety mentor, and friend for many years. Between the covers of this book, he has distilled many complex safety concepts learned over decades of safety leadership into down-to-earth, easily understandable safety truths. These simple truths, if applied daily, will help both the individual employee reader or a larger company group to have an injury-free workplace and lifestyle. His book is useful both to the safety professional and to the newest employee on the job."

—**DON ADKINS**,
Vice President, Safety and Training, Davis H. Elliot Co., Inc.

Contents

Foreword

As leaders, we work extremely hard to help our organizations prevent unwanted events. While we hold great faith in our programs, policies and procedures, we still fear the day of receiving a phone call notifying us someone was significantly injured on the job. When this has occurred in the past, I find myself looking in the mirror and asking, "What could I have done differently? What could our team have done differently?" Safety failures are leadership failures and anyone who has served in this line of work knows the feeling.

Over the years, I have often sought wise counsel to help bolster the safety performance of our company. My hope was to find the right people, at the right times, to add value to our team and improve our culture. When I think back on those who I have leaned on, Ken Sheridan immediately comes to mind.

After meeting Ken over 20 years ago, it was apparent his passion, knowledge, and ability to communicate effectively was impactful. Seeing how he was able to influence from the crew level to the Executive team was impressive. I admired the way he spoke about safety, culture, and the value of protecting your teammates through his concept of "No Compromise." It was refreshing to hear someone talk about safety the way he did. His passion clearly came from a place of care, but he also understood the role safety played in maintaining a healthy business and brand. Ken told me, "You must manage safety the same as you manage your profitability." Upon learning of his retirement from a utility company, I knew he would be a great addition to our company.

During this period, we were continuing to improve our safety performance at Elliot, and we had built an incredible foundation of servant leaders who were hungry to reach our goal of Target Zero. I knew the more people we could bring into the fold to fuel this fire, the better off we would be. Ken fit the bill. From the moment he joined our Elliot Family, Ken made an impact. Whether it was through his weekly No Compromise Moment video series which injected his enthusiasm into the hearts and minds of our employees, or the conversations he would have with the leaders at every level in our organization about developing the necessary mindset to reach the levels of success we strived for, he added value.

When Ken initially approached me about writing a book, I couldn't help but think of the lives he would change through his words. I saw, firsthand, how the safety truths he spoke about so frequently could power positive change, and I had no doubt it was a message which required a larger audience.

I'm thankful for Ken's friendship, guidance, and expertise. He has truly had a positive impact on me personally, and so many of us professionally. I hope this book helps everyone who reads it to not only be a better leader in their organization, but a better leader in every area of their life. However, understand, getting to this point will require you to never waiver, never doubt yourself, and most importantly, never compromise along the way.

—DAVID HASKINS,
President/CEO, Davis H. Elliot Company, Inc.

Introduction

When I began telling people I had written a book, they often asked how long the process took. The answer is simple: It's taken a lifetime. I've spent nearly all of my adult life working alongside blue- and white-collar professionals in the electrical powerline industry, and each and every one contributed to my desire and visceral need to get all of us home safe and intact at the end of the day. Now, as I enter the latter years of my career, I want to share my hard-learned truths with the next generation of C-suite occupants; line technicians, field supervisors, and journeymen; and department heads, safety leaders and HR professionals, all of whom play a significant role in workplace safety.

Like most people, my career path was a bit winding, but each experience allowed me to gather the skills needed to shift peoples' perception of safety and to develop the No Compromise philosophy. I learned how to protect myself as a young man in law enforcement and corrections, developed the speaking and motivation skills necessary to mentor and coach, and received a thorough, life-saving education in the importance of safety in utility and construction work. Through these experiences, I found myself able to connect and communicate effectively with most anybody, whether they're from the city or from my neck of the Kentucky woods, those from prestigious universities and the young men and women just entering the trades.

Through these experiences and conversations with people of all backgrounds, I was able to identify and construct core fundamental traits for companies that have or desire to have a strong safety culture, from the boardroom to the bucket truck.

Whether you are the person calling the shots in the corner office or you spend your time working in the elements to get the job done under less-than-ideal conditions, these safety truths will provide important insights into how you conduct your work without sacrificing efficiency and safety.

Before you read this book, some points that may not seem to be applicable to you at this point in your career, but it is important for you to understand the entire operation of your company and how everyone has ownership in building a strong culture of No Compromise. If you're working in the field, you should understand what types of decisions those back in the office juggle on a daily basis. It is easy to say, "Why should I care about what the vice president thinks?" Recognize that person is responsible for budgets, revenue, maintenance, equipment, and so much more. The decisions they make and their responsibilities directly impact you and your ability to do your work safely and to the best of your abilities.

If you're an executive, you may be tempted to gloss over a section that seems targeted to those working at the mid- or entry-level positions of your company. I strongly encourage you to avoid falling into that trap. It is vital to your organizational success to truly understand what your employees need from you, and how you have influence in the lives of each individual working for your company. After all, we all share the same responsibility—making sure every single person can make a good living, support their family, and return home each night in the same condition they left for work.

Safety and operations must be permanently intertwined as communication and knowledge is woven throughout a successful organization. Understanding how each piece of the puzzle fits together benefits everyone. The more safety champions you have in your company, the stronger you will be, and the stronger you are, the more successful your organization will become. Once you have a critical mass of employees supporting and actively engaged in a culture of safety, your organization will grow and prosper. While no one can guarantee having all the pieces in the right place will keep your company free from incidents, I can say with confidence these truths are the best way to build the lowest risk work environment.

Ultimately, this is what inspired me to write this book. I think back to the people who influenced my behavior and mindset regarding safety in my early days, the people who regularly work and lead with safety ideals in their job, and those who choose to embrace and implement the No Compromise approach into their businesses. I have been fortunate to work with many great people and serve several great companies during my career, such as Louisville Gas & Electric and KU Energy, and the Davis H. Elliot Company. It is because of these organizations, and all who work there, that I could influence others in a positive manner. I always wanted to do what I could to keep them safe, and my drive to get everyone home in one piece made my career feel like it was far more than just a paycheck.

The second question I often get after being asked how long it took me the write the book is this: "Am I going to be in it?" Unfortunately, this question is much harder to answer, and a bit disappointing. As you read the book, you will realize I was influenced by men and women at practically every turn. As a result, I have an overwhelming appreciation and respect for not only the high-consequence, high-risk workers, but also for those who make it possible for me to have climbed that pole, from both a lineman perspective and a career perspective. There are human resources leaders and staffers who taught me about united goals in seemingly disparate departments, grizzled, quiet field supervisors who taught me to listen, vice presidents who lead with their hearts and youngsters who taught me the gift of learning. Through them, I figured out that everyone can be a teacher—sometimes in less than positive ways— and that it's up to me to learn. To all of you, I thank you.

More personally, I look at my grandson. He has begun his career in the same industry I spent so many years in. I'm proud to see him doing this work, and I'm thankful he will be one of many who will continue in the proud tradition of linework. I intimately understand the risks everyone who chooses this career is taking, and I want to do everything I can to protect him and them.

I encourage you to look out for your coworkers, your employees, your bosses, and those you work with from other companies on projects or in response to storms and catastrophes. Think about their families, learn what they care about, and make the choice to lead with safety to safeguard what they love. Be your brothers' and sisters' keeper.

If you follow these truths, you will be the cornerstone of a safety culture that will transform this industry and affect lives for the better in perpetuity. This top-led, employee-driven approach will develop safety champions throughout the company and build a low-risk safety culture that is second to none. Safety is more than statistics, data, and metrics; it's a way of life and the foundation of a thriving business.

History will repeat itself unless you make a change.

We naturally perform the same patterns of behavior unless we make a conscious effort to change. Without a behavior change, the result stays the same.

The definition of insanity is doing the same thing over and over and expecting a different result.

—*Einstein, allegedly*

The best near-miss I ever had.

I was born and raised in Caldwell County in western Kentucky. I left home to attend Murray State University in Murray, KY, where I crammed four years of college into four-and-a-half years, majoring in health and physical education with a minor in sociology. My original plan was to be a high school teacher and a football and wrestling coach but since I graduated in the middle of the academic year, I could not get hired. I had to find something to do.

I ended up working at the Kentucky State Penitentiary.

I worked there for a total of six months. I was initially hired as a correctional counselor but the penitentiary human resources department first wanted to expose me to the security aspects of working in a prison. Fierce fights and killings were not unusual; I witnessed four of these violent events in my short time there. I'd never been around anything like it, and I hated the job. When I look back, however, I realize that job was the beginning of my journey in safety.

One day they told me, "Sheridan, we'd like for you to take this inmate from Eddyville over to Madisonville," which was a forty-five-minute drive to the northeast. The prison did not have the medical facilities the man required, and he needed transport to a civilian hospital. "I'd be glad to," I said. The inmate weighed about 160 pounds, and I weighed around 220 at the time. When I went to get him, I sized him up, decided he wasn't much of a physical threat, and thought, "This is gonna be a piece of cake." He couldn't overpower me. The odds were in my favor that I wasn't going to have a problem with him.

The inmate and I had to pass through three security doors to get outside the prison walls. We walked through the first set, and at the second, I chained him up so he couldn't escape. First, I wrapped a chain around his waist, then handcuffed him and attached the handcuffs to the chain. Finally, I shackled his legs. Given our size difference and his restraints, I figured he was no threat. As he shuffled outside behind me, I watched him look around, eyes as big as saucers, and I heard him softly say, "Whoa." It had been a long time since he had seen anything around him but prison walls.

As we approached the number one wall stand, the officer posted there said, "Sheridan, here's your gun." "I don't want a gun," I replied, to which he answered, "Sheridan, it's standard operating procedure. You will take a gun."

"I'm not gonna shoot anybody. Why do you want me to take a gun?"

"No questions," he replied. "There's no way you're leaving here without a gun." I took the gun grudgingly and dropped it, holster and all, in my pants pocket. I was determined not to attach the holster and gun to my belt. This man in chains was no threat to me, he couldn't take off running, and I felt an internal pang that told me I could never take another person's life.

The inmate and I went down the stairs to the state car, and the driver jumped out, pitched me the keys, and wished me good luck. I caught them, opened the back door, and the inmate slid in. Once I settled into the driver's seat, I realized a plexiglass screen was all we had between us was. I thought, "I've still got the day made. I've got one person to guard, a nice drive ahead, and it's a gorgeous Kentucky July day." We left the prison and headed out to Madisonville.

Less than two miles from the penitentiary, my dad-blame gun dropped out of my pocket, fell between the seats, and landed right between the inmate's feet. I don't know what most people would have done in this situation, but I hit the brakes with all I could muster. It was the 1970s, and seatbelts weren't required or even used very often. As I slammed the brakes, I looked up in the mirror and saw the inmate's face approaching fast. He hit that Plexiglass with a bam and fell back into his seat, the gun still between his feet. I threw the car into park, opened the door, and took off in a sprint, leaving my car running. As I ran up a nearby hill, I heard myself yelling, "Don't you touch that gun! Don't you touch that gun!" After I made it to the top of the hill, I thought, "Now, what am I going to do?"

Well, the inmate thought I looked pretty funny, and he started laughing. "This may not be so bad," I thought. He waved me back, and I started coming down the hill. When I got about halfway there, he bent down like he was going to grab the gun. I jumped up and started running up the hill again. July in Kentucky can be hot, so by the time I'd run up and down that hill a couple times, I was working up a good sweat.

Each time a car would pass, I would turn around and pretend like I was picking blackberries, trying to hide the fact that I'd just made the most basic prison guard mistake ever—my car was running, an inmate was shackled and handcuffed in the back seat, and he had my weapon. Once the car went by, he'd smile and wave me down. Then he'd lean forward like he was going to pick up my gun, so I'd run back up.

After several rounds of his version of fun, he finally let me come down. Back at the car, I had to reach between that man's feet to grab my gun and holster off the floor, a dangerous move even with the man in shackles. This time, I put the holster and gun on my belt as instructed in the first place. As we drove away, the inmate said, "I tell you what, Sheridan, I won't tell anybody if you won't." And we didn't. I never told anybody about that near-miss until I was long gone from the Kentucky State Penitentiary.

Poor safety performance will repeat itself unless you make a change.

That near-miss taught me a lot about safety, mainly that I never wanted to surrender my weapon to an inmate ever again. I also learned that the lowest risk method for carrying a pistol is to place the gun in a holster and secure the holster on your belt. To prevent incidents from reoccurring, we need to figure out what changes to make, and have the courage and motivation to realize those changes and the initiative to sustain them.

Reporting near-misses is one way to determine what changes we need to make and communicating them to others ensures safety for everyone. There's no better time to learn how to prevent a near-miss or incident from recurring than right after it happens. The problem is getting people to openly communicate near misses because they may be embarrassed by their actions. Instead of telling somebody about it, it's much easier to say, like the inmate, "This was our problem, we fixed it, and nobody needs to know anything about it." This mantra is broadly known as "what happens in our crew, stays in our crew."

I know firsthand how that feels. Just like prison officers know they need a weapon when moving an inmate, every apprentice lineman knows electricity always seeks a path to ground. When I was a line technician, I made a fundamental mistake any person allowed on a pole knows not to make. I was working on a crew changing out a 40-foot power pole to a 45-foot power pole with 12,000 volts of potential difference, a task I had done many times before. First, I worked my way to the top of the pole and isolated all the grounds to eliminate the potential for a phase-to-ground contact with energized conductors. As I transferred the outside phase, I covered it up with a rubber hose to isolate it and then worked my way to the middle. It was at the middle phase when I had a near-miss—I accidentally dropped the conductor. There was a slight angle on the pole location, which created an angle on the phase. When I lost control, it caused the conductor to bounce and go sideways toward the outside phase. I just knew we were about to have a phase-to-phase contact, potentially causing a fire, an explosion, an unintended outage, or even my own death.

Even though this slip only took a split second, time stood still. I could see the conductor falling in slow motion, but I couldn't stop it. I knew if it hit another energized line, I would be toast. All I could do at that moment was brace myself for a high-temperature arc flash or contact with the out-of-control energized conductor that could find a path to ground through my body. Fortunately, when the energized conductor landed, it was in the clear, and a life-threatening crisis was averted.

My boss told me to come down. As I lowered my bucket 45 feet to the ground, I thought, "Oh boy, he's gonna chew me out." I was embarrassed because I failed the transmission and distribution industry's number one fundamental safety practice: Always maintain control of energized equipment. When I reached the ground, we talked about what went wrong, and he said, "Get your wits before you go back up. Right after a near-miss is a time when there's an increased risk of another incident." Later, we shared the near-miss with other crews and emphasized using extreme focus on the task at hand, especially when doing hot work.

It would have been so easy to keep that event within our own crew. Every apprentice, journeyman, and foreman trains doggedly on the importance of and the necessary steps to maintain 100% control of the energized equipment they are working on and anything that can make contact with it. I didn't relish the idea of telling everyone I made such an elementary mistake. It would have been much easier to say nothing about it, and nobody would be the wiser. The smarter and much harder thing to do would be to learn from our experience by figuring out the root cause of the near-miss and share it with the entire team so everyone in the organization could work to prevent a similar recurrence.

It's natural to wonder why it is necessary to make a big deal over something that didn't actually happen. Two reasons come to mind: A lack of action produces results as much as an action, and history *will* repeat itself unless you make a change. Even if nothing happens to you in a near-miss event, you need to learn from the experience, and you have a fundamental obligation to share it with others. Considering the law of averages, a higher frequency of the same behavior will lead to a higher percentage of that event turning into a full-blown accident. I cannot imagine how terrible I would feel if I didn't report my experience in hot pole work, and the same kind of mistake ended up killing someone else.

Summary of Safety Truth #1: History will repeat itself unless you make a change.

Looking at our history gives us the benefit of hindsight. The further we go back in time, the more the trends will mean to us. Understanding the historical safety data in our organization gives us the insight to forecast the future and make positive changes. To identify changes to make, look for opportunities to improve safety behaviors by providing specific training, strengthening policies, and establishing open and effective communication. Like the quote often misattributed to Einstein, we need to dig into past operational standards that were not correctly taught or applied. In a No Compromise Safety Culture, we fully understand that poor safety performance can repeat itself *anywhere* in the organization. It's not just one location. It's not a jinx. It's not luck. It's an accumulation of how well we apply these truths.

Safety is good business.

Safety is a crucial business component of any high-risk industry with high-cost consequences. Organizations that build safety into their business planning metrics experience greater financial success and growth in every area.

The first time I said safety is a good business decision, I received a lot of pushback. They said, "Sheridan, you can't say that. You can't talk about safety and dollars in the same breath."

"Why not?" I asked. "Who cares what drives a world-class safety culture? Having one is a win for everyone."

When you are running a business, good safety performance is crucial for success. We should all be proud to work for a company that values safety and considers a No Compromise Safety Culture their best business decision. In the construction industry, safety is sometimes considered to be about the people and *only* about the people. It has been taboo to associate safety and incident prevention with profits because employees might negatively interpret that to mean safety is about cutting incidents to save money on employee medical care. Of course, this is not true. A well-run organization knows taking care of people always takes priority over profits. The safety of employees, subcontractors, and the public must be everyone's goal, and we should not be ashamed to say safety is good business. The two need not be separated. There is nothing wrong with associating safety performance with making money in an organization; it is not difficult to see that a company with a poor safety performance will not sustain profits.

Where does the safety department fit into the company structure?

Safety is a corporate responsibility that can fall under more than one business area. Some organizations have safety professionals reporting to human resources. The common thinking behind this setup is that all things employee-related should fall under human resources. Over the years, I have seen safety departments operate more effectively under the operations umbrella. Our safety goal is to create the lowest risk environment possible, and operations oversees the area of the company with the highest risk. We want safety to collaborate closely with human resources and internal communications, as well as other departments. Placing safety under operations, however, opens the door for creating a long-term, sustainable safety culture.

Good safety performance plays a significant role in defining the success of a company.

When we value safety by including it in every aspect of the business, it's a win for everyone in all departments. In fact, integrating safety into all aspects of the business provides an increased profit margin while positively impacting employees. If we looked across the construction industry and compared company profits to safety records, I guarantee we'd see a correlation. Businesses with poor safety results—higher incident rates and fatalities—predictably have lower profits and negatively impact employees and their families.

It isn't easy to quantify the actual cost of an incident because there are so many hidden costs. The most apparent costs include medical care and lost time, damage or loss of product, repairs to facilities and equipment, overtime pay and temporary labor, unit delays, investigation time, regulatory and legal costs, loss of contracts, and damage to business relationships. In addition, there are other less obvious costs, such as more expensive insurance premiums due to increased Experience Modification Rates (EMRs), increased cost of hiring and training replacements, decreased efficiency of temporary employees, recruiting challenges, and loss of business and goodwill.

No company has unlimited resources. When an organization uses funds to pay for all costs associated with an incident, it takes that money away from operations, capital improvements, investments in employees, and shareholders. When managing your personal finances, what budget do you take from to cover an unexpected cost? Are you spending money to repair something you damaged yourself? Do you have to take money out of your vacation fund to pay for it?

The company's business plan should include safety.

In business planning, safety should be viewed as an asset, a value proposition, and a business driver that supports the company's vision, mission, and strategy. Everyone in the organization should see safety as an integral part of the business plan and include safety targets alongside financial targets in measuring success. This planning begins at the top of the organization and cascades down the chain of command. Every person in a leadership role looks strategically at how they achieve safety results. Frontline leaders begin each day's work by planning ways to achieve safety goals.

Integrate safety into all business areas.

It's not intuitive for all departments to include safety in their strategic plans, but the result is synergistic when they do. Safety should be part of the budget, personnel, and planning programs that comprise the business plan because those elements are integral parts of the company culture. In a No Compromise Safety Culture, everyone in the organization adopts a safety mindset. They think about safety first and throughout. They always ask, "How does safety relate to this objective, project, job bid, or policy change?"

For a No Compromise Safety Culture to work, we need design engineers, human resources departments, contract administrators, inspectors, procurement staff, fleet managers, and other departments thinking about safety *before* it gets to the operations department. Divisions must understand how their role connects to safety and how their team impacts operational outcomes. For example, when the human resources department incorporates safety into all job descriptions, they help create safety expectations for every person in the organization. Similarly, managers should consider safety in their hiring practices and promotion decisions. Each employee should understand that safety standards come with their role and department and how those standards interact with other departments.

In NASCAR, you cannot win a race with just a fast engine. You need a skilled driver, a talented pit crew, good fuel, and so on. No single element ever gets the job done. When we look at each area in our organization, we continually discover new ways for each department to develop a No Compromise Safety Culture. For example, during a catastrophic ice storm, our procurement department completed the first safety screening of potential restoration crews before we completed the contracts. Initiating this step *before* we committed to hiring these contractors ensured our safety standards remained intact and that the contractors fully understood our organizational commitment to safety. Our procurement partners accomplished this win because our No Compromise approach was integrated into their daily work, and they understood it, embraced it, and actualized it.

You cannot buy safety.

The first step to creating a No Compromise Safety Culture is to decide to do it. Over the years, I have seen plenty of examples of leaders who set aside money to purchase an off-the-shelf safety program. These leaders would never dream of buying an off-the-shelf business plan; why would they think an off-the-shelf safety program would work? In the same way a business plan is specific to a company's financial goals, a No Compromise Safety Culture should be specific to the organization's safety goals. Creating a low-risk work environment requires time and hard work. It takes a top-led, employee-driven approach that requires extensive communication and coordination. Many change agents trust sociology theories such as the Hawthorne Theory, which refers to the concept that if you become aware of an undesirable behavior, you will take the steps needed to modify that behavior. Additionally, if you begin to measure and track your progress in anything—exercise, diet, budgeting, work processes—you begin to see improved results.

Summary of Safety Truth #2: Safety is good business.

Incorporating a No Compromise Safety Culture into all aspects of the business gives organizations more opportunities to be successful than any other business management tool. When safety is part of the business plan, the value for safety starts at the top, which leads to positive impacts throughout the organization. In addition to having healthier, happier employees, safety-focused organizations make more money that can be applied to retirement funds, bonuses, pay increases, and new equipment. Employees enjoy greater job security, and CEOs and leaders have more of a chance to grow the company. Profit margins are larger, employee relations are better, and incident and insurance costs are lower and more efficient. Business is better because the entire organization is driving success through safety. What better claim to fame can you have than being able to say your business values a low-risk, high-reward business model?

The safety model that works best is top-led and employee-driven.

_____

The leadership of an organization sets the culture in motion. The behaviors and goals they prioritize filter through the company and become the behaviors and goals of employees.

Safety begins with the CEO.

For a No Compromise Safety Culture model to work, it must come from the top of the organization. Does the CEO demonstrate a personal value of integrating safety as a way to run the company? If top leaders value safety, the entire organization is well on its way to building a culture of No Compromise.

Senior leaders who drive a No Compromise Safety Culture take advantage of opportunities to lead visibly with safety. They understand the importance of talking about safety with the same level of passion and urgency they emphasize when discussing return on investment, human capital management, functional goals, and other performance metrics. They communicate and demonstrate intentional values for safety by integrating elevated safety metrics into business and operational performance. Everyone in the organization sees this commitment to safety, and this safety-focused behavior filters down through the middle managers, foremen, crew leaders, and crew members in a positive way.

A No Compromise Safety Culture requires effective, open communication.

To demonstrate your personal value for safety, you need to show your intent in your words and actions. This intent begins with consistently clear and direct, effective communication.

When I was working as a safety professional in the utility industry, I witnessed a moment that told me our No Compromise Safety Culture was gaining traction. One of our top senior vice presidents (SVPs) opened a contractor meeting with, "There's an evil driver amongst us, and that is money. Let there be no doubt. If anyone here has a misguided perception that you can make more money by compromising safety, you better know that's not how we do business."

When a senior leader communicates a directive clearly, as this SVP did with safety, the result is powerful. This endorsement from the top became the foundation of our No Compromise Safety Culture. We quoted his statement for years as we continued to incorporate safe work practices and procedures. The focus on safety integrated into profits became an internal brand for our organization. It lifted employee morale and productivity, reduced incidents, and increased profit margins. We collaborated with the corporate communications department, and they integrated this quote into internal and external communication material. And nobody questioned its validity. In fact, the statement was so strong and so well communicated it became part of our standard operating procedures.

Leading with safety.

We cannot simply say, "We want zero incidents today," and expect it to happen magically. We must lead with safety and have the protocols and policies to back it up 100% of the time.

There are many ways for senior leaders to demonstrate a personal value of safety through their role. One example is to begin meetings with safety. Some people may ask, "How will starting a leadership meeting with safety prevent an incident in the field?" and the answer is simple: Leading with safety is proactive. It's an opportunity to identify and prevent threats and to recognize achievements. Talking about it at leadership meetings endorses safety and mandates we perform our work in a certain way. When safety is the focus throughout the organization, it takes away the risk of cutting corners because it sets the tone for how we work.

Have courage!

Courage is crucial for creating a top-led, employee-driven safety model. To make a significant change in anything, you must have the courage to speak up when others are silent, ask difficult questions, and show your vulnerability. For example, a frontline leader requested a piece of machinery to pull in a wire. Before ordering the equipment, the general foreman asked if anyone on the crew had experience using the specific brand. Nobody had used that brand before, so the general foreman decided to provide an operator with the equipment. The general foreman lowered risk by providing an experienced operator while adding job training and development for the crew. They dared to speak up to identify and control a potential hazard.

Everyone in the organization—no matter what position—needs support and courage to perform at the highest level. Everyone must feel empowered to speak up or call a stop to unsafe work. We want each and every person to feel comfortable asking questions and saying they understand—or, more importantly, that they *don't* understand—a function, a piece of equipment, a desired outcome, or an expectation. Each person needs the courage to own their work and assume a leadership role before one is formally assigned to them, and everyone needs the courage to do what they know is right, even if it's unpopular.

All these behaviors depend on the actions of company leadership. Leaders must foster an atmosphere of open communication and respect by developing keen listening, observation, and communication skills. They must model how they want others to behave in the organization. A No Compromise Safety Culture at its core allows employees to learn—to have coworkers and leaders alike saying, "It's okay not to know everything." When asking questions and learning are a normal part of the day, both new and seasoned employees feel valued and recognized. Teams work better together. Projects come together faster. Organizations transform the quality and safety of their work while building an inclusive culture. Ultimately, the real test of a No Compromise Safety Culture is when *everyone* in the organization is comfortable enough in the work environment to show courage.

Is backing into parking spaces truly necessary?

Backing into parking spaces is a known safety method. Most construction companies have a policy requiring drivers to back into parking spaces instead of driving forward into spaces. It is well-documented that backing into a parking spot upon arrival is safer than pulling in because the driver's focus on their surroundings. Backing in immediately may prove easier than backing out later with potentially more vehicles and distractions in the area. It is easy to do; it's also easy to ignore.

One time, a senior leader visited our office for a few days. On the first day, roughly half the cars in the parking lot were backed into spaces as mandated by policy. The executive carefully backed his car into a parking space and entered the building. The next day, all but two cars aligned with the backing policy. By the final day of his visit, all the vehicles complied with the back-in policy. Everyone thought the executive had mentioned our parking policy to someone, who passed the comment around the office, but nobody ever heard him say it. He didn't have to say it. His actions spoke for him. True leaders execute safety policies to facilitate the normalization of standard operating procedures. The payoff for adhering to the parking policy is much more than a financial benefit. It's a significant cultural win.

How many safety professionals does it take?

When companies hire me to help them create a No Compromise Safety Culture, the first thing they do is show me the safety team and inevitably point out how many safety professionals they have per employee. Some seem to think that if you have a lot of safety professionals, you will automatically have a world-class safety program. Is it the number of safety professionals that makes your safety culture? Absolutely not. It's the line leadership. Line management leads and supports safety. Line leaders are the men and women who make the company run; they are paid to produce the product, and they must embrace the concept that safety supports the bottom line.

The employees drive safety.

Safety is led by organizational leadership, but it's driven and kept alive by the employees. Decision-makers must listen closely to the people doing the work and managing hazards. These employees have a focused view of what needs to be done in the field to operate. They will identify problems you never knew existed and offer solutions you might never otherwise consider.

Whenever you tool up company equipment, the first consideration should always be the end user. When the Occupational Safety and Health Administration (OSHA) changed climbing safety procedures from free climbing to requiring 100% fall protection for all climbing, our organization needed to purchase special equipment to comply with the new mandate. We asked our line technicians to select two options of climbing gear that would help them do their jobs as safely as possible. They chose, and the company budgeted for and purchased the equipment the line technicians recommended. Giving the line technicians power over this procurement decision served us well. In addition to investing in the most appropriate equipment for the task, we showed our employees that we respect their knowledge, experiences, and opinions.

The No-Gap Philosophy.

The No-Gap Philosophy is about making sure there are no gaps in the flow of communication from the top leaders to the individual contributor. Our goal is to prevent these gaps with concrete objectives, proper training, and clear communication. In the

No-Gap Philosophy, each person in the company contributes to and directly impacts a No Compromise Safety Culture.

Everyone begins to ask, "How can we integrate safety into our work to achieve the company's goals? Have we considered safety in all aspects of this plan?" In our work lives, we perform to the expectations of our boss, and our boss performs to the expectations of their boss, and so on. We rarely exceed those expectations, and we don't usually break the chain of command. As a result, the foreman or crew leader is the leader of a thriving safety culture. Conversely, if someone's boss doesn't support a No Compromise Safety Culture, that person may let it slide.

A policy that comes from the top of the organization sets the tone for safety, but the frontline leaders make it happen. When leadership effectively demonstrates and communicates safety in the organization but it is not producing the desired results, one needs to look for the gap. What level of management is not performing? At what level is the breakdown in communication and demonstration occurring? Is it between you and the person performing the work?

Each hierarchical layer has a role to play in a successful performance. The current will not flow to the next level if there is a gap, and neither will a No Compromise Safety Culture. When we have a breakdown, we need to find the gap, figure out why it is happening, and fix it.

Gaining momentum

Once my organization started rolling out a No Compromise Safety Culture and reduced our incidents *and* our expenses, leaders and employees all over the company realized what a solid safety program we had created. In addition to the leadership team endorsing No Compromise, we saw supervisors, crew leaders, and linemen adopting it as well. As a result of our employees driving our safety program, we started applying for and receiving awards. Everyone in our industry heard about our achievements as safety leaders, and we communicated our success internally and externally, giving our employees full credit for making it happen. The women and men in our company were proud of their success and felt valued. We had successfully created an expectation where everyone felt ownership for our safety culture and worked to maintain it.

Four parts of a successful safety model

To work, No Compromise must be a critical part of an organization's culture. It's not optional, and it's not half-baked. It's the basis on which you run the business. You must live and breathe in a top-led, employee-driven approach to safety.

The four fundamental parts are:

1. **Safety begins at the top of the organization.** Senior leaders must communicate and demonstrate their commitment to a No Compromise Safety Culture and use that commitment to drive all business decisions.

2. **Frontline leaders manage and support the success of a No Compromise Safety Culture.** Frontline leaders have *the most significant* influence on employee behaviors. They set the expectations for a No Compromise Safety Culture with decisive leadership, demonstration of proper practices, and unwavering commitment.

3. **Everyone, including contractors, must understand the safety management process.** Any time you give your employees or business partners accountability for any aspect of operations, they must first take charge of safety.

4. **Employees drive the approach to safety.** Employee engagement and commitment is the secret sauce that binds concentrated efforts to identify potential hazards and proactively addresses them before they become injuries.

When a focus on safety begins at the top, everyone in the organization begins to shift into a safety mindset. Employees start to drive safely by incorporating it into their daily work. Everyone asks, "What does it take for us to complete today's tasks safely?" This concept applies to everything—from how we handle a pandemic like COVID-19 to how the fleet department chooses the safest vehicles. If the company uses contractors, hiring managers understand the need to implement processes to ensure contractors adopt an expectation of safety above all else. When everyone begins to recognize that their success or failure is based on safety results, they begin to incorporate safety into everything they do.

Summary of Safety Truth #3: The safety model that works best is top-led and employee-driven.

Once the CEO and leadership team have established safety as a non-negotiable value, senior management can ensure they have the right people in the right roles to drive safety in all parts of the organization. Instead of rushing to place the not-quite-right-for-job internal person in a specific position, they may decide to recruit from outside the company to hire the individual who better meets the job requirements. As the executive team sees the positive results of No Compromise implementation, moving forward in safety falls into place in an easy, predictable way. From there, other aspects of the business succeed because managing safety is the same process it takes to manage all the different components of our business. Safety becomes ingrained in everyone's daily work, and that's a win for everybody.

As goes the frontline leader, so goes safety.

Frontline leaders are the go-to influencers in the company. Their job is to influence the technical professionals to ensure a No Compromise Safety Culture pervades every task and operation.

Frontline leaders carry much responsibility.

We've talked about how important it is for senior leaders to lead with safety and for employees to drive safety. How are the two connected? Through the frontline leader, who is arguably the most critical person in the company when it comes to influencing culture. They are the conduit connecting upper management to field-based employees. All roles are important, but if the frontline leader does not support an action, there's a good chance it will not get done.

As the supervisor, the frontline leader will spend more energy than anybody else making sure the job gets done safely. Not only do they need to be technically proficient, but they must also be able to manage projects and people. Frontline leaders catch everything from the top, from OSHA regulations to company policies. They interpret and condense this information into actions to administer the job and oversee the crew. Newly promoted frontline leaders already know how to build a three-phase transformer bank and make the rotations rotate any way they want, but now they need to develop an equally effective management style. For this reason, choosing the right person as a frontline leader role is paramount.

Get the right person in the role.

Frontline leaders are often caught between a rock and a hard place in which they must carefully weigh outcomes and choose between two equally unpleasant actions. It's a big job usually awarded to a line technician who has successfully demonstrated a highly technical set of skills. Unfortunately, the unintended consequence is that we sometimes promote technically talented people into frontline leader positions who lack experience leading teams. The result is often a newly promoted line technician who may not understand the safety truths that drive a culture of No Compromise.

Many frontline leaders teach and lead in the same manner they experienced as up-and-comers. If their previous managers didn't groom them to someday manage, they might not be immediately effective in this new role. A lucky few frontline leaders can intuitively learn things like productivity measures, but we don't want them to learn the importance of safety the hard way—through near misses and incidents. In safety, we cannot afford to have injuries as a learning mechanism. No matter how productive a crew is, if incidents or near misses occur during the process, the outcome is unacceptable.

Cultivate the frontline leader.

In the transmission and distribution industry, we have many opportunities to learn the craft on the job. Our formal apprenticeship programs effectively bring a person up through the ranks from ground person to line technician and beyond.

When it comes to future frontline leaders, however, we often miss the opportunity to groom today's line technicians for the next role. In today's unpredictable world, an experienced line technician may start the week working on a pole and end the week as a newly promoted frontline leader.

To prepare a line technician to be an outstanding frontline leader, we need a methodology to explain, train, and develop this person for the role of a supervisor. Luckily, the chance to share knowledge doesn't have to be a formal training program;

it can be a gradual progression in responsibility, such as coaching a new hire, leading a job briefing, or planning how to approach a complex project. For the newly promoted frontline leader, it can be daily conversations about what worked and what didn't. For the seasoned frontline leader, it can be grooming the next line technician to be a frontline leader by pulling this person aside a few minutes each day to share insights.

Make safety stick.

Ask a typical crew, "What are you billing this job on? Units or time and material?" I'm willing to bet everyone will know the answer. Now ask them, "What is the voltage on this line?" or "Which way does this line feed?" It is possible somebody may not know the answers. It's essential to understand the business side of the operation—after all, we are working to make a living. In a No Compromise Safety Culture, everyone on the crew should also understand the details about safety on a job site, and it's the frontline leader's job to make sure of this.

Understand your role as the frontline leader.

As a frontline leader, your primary role is to *lead*. Depending on the job, this role can take on many different responsibilities. Two skills you must bring to the game as a frontline leader are technical expertise and a sense of managing people, also known as leadership skills. Your technical expertise will guide you as you oversee the completion of the job most safely. You will determine the steps your crew takes in each phase of the work and the best way to prevent incidents during each task. Your technical leadership skills will help you do the job, and your leadership skills will guide you to make sure your team completes the operation safely. Both are equally important; it's not enough to simply tell the team you want a safe day's work. You must understand how to create an environment where safety and technical skills are conjoined.

Nine ways to excel as a frontline leader.

What do frontline leaders need to do to be successful in this role? First, they need to understand the nine safety truths in this book. Then, to be truly exceptional as a frontline leader, they also need to implement the nine frontline leader guiding principles below.

1. THINK IT, PLAN IT, EXECUTE IT, AND FOLLOW-UP ON IT.

According to *Inc.* magazine, most adults make about 35,000 decisions a day. From deciding when to roll out of bed in the morning to when to turn off the bedside lamp at night, we observe, process, and act over and over throughout the day. In the transmission and distribution industry, our decisions have powerful ramifications. For the frontline leader to create a foundation for a low-risk environment, every decision must be calculated and purposeful. The best way to lead a safe operation is to think, plan, execute, and follow-up on your work.

Think. Think first. Plan out the operation and the entire day. Consider your available human and mechanical capabilities. Draw on your training and experience to make decisions about how to complete a job safely.

If you need help, ask for it, and encourage your team to ask the same of you. OSHA regulations require a briefing before starting every job for this very reason. A safety conversation flushes out areas of confidence and potential hurdles and creates an opportunity to identify and problem-solve without risk to life and property. Without thinking about safety first, we can't adequately address all the aspects of even the most straightforward job.

Plan. Planning your work takes on a new level of importance when you become a frontline leader. Before starting all jobs, collaborate with your team as you ask common safety questions. What are the proper procedures to use for this task? What safety protection do we need for this task? Gloves and sleeves? Proper cover? Fall protection? Does everyone have this equipment, and is it in good working order?

Execute. Safe execution starts with effective communication. Never assume everyone on the team knows what you're thinking and what they need to do. Comprehensively use your knowledge base to recall any safety issues that happened to others doing this particular task. Be fully present and engaged in the activity.

Follow-up. After each job, bring everyone together to talk about what worked and why. Encourage the crew to participate in the conversation by communicating openly and without judgment. Ask open-ended questions instead of questions that can be answered with "yes" or "no."

Remember, how you react to incidents is nearly as important as what happened. Gather all facts. Determine the critical aspects and what needs to be changed to get a different result. Make the necessary change to prevent future recurrences. Communicate clearly and directly about what needs to change next time.

2. MANAGE SAFETY BASED ON THE POSITIVES.

To be an effective leader in safety, seek and communicate the positive in everything you do. It can be hard to overcome negative comments and their impact. By no means should you ignore the negative or avoid addressing problems. Instead, it means you should identify the positive and reinforce it. Reinforcement could be as simple as a high five or a handshake; it could be praise or public recognition or having a cookout for the crew. One safety professional I know cooks and serves breakfast to his team to celebrate wins.

When you address issues, you should identify and handle them immediately. Above all, take your role as a liaison to upper management seriously. They rely on your support the same way you rely on your crew's support. Consistently deliver news and information from upper management in a positive light. Your team will take your lead on how to interpret and react to it. When given responsibility for others, a positive attitude can make you successful. Simply put, if something's good, keep telling your team it's good.

Understand the law and know how to follow it.

"Keep your eye on the ball" is the best advice for almost every sport, and it's valid for safety as well. If you don't start your meeting off with safety and integrate safety into each task or talk more about units and work production than safety, you're taking your eye off the safety goal. Most people already know the OSHA restrictions that govern the construction industry. They can even recite parts of OSHA's 1910.269 safety code. Does this make a great safety leader? You certainly need to know the rules, and it's even more important to understand how to enforce them.

3. CORRECT UNSAFE OR UNHEALTHY ACTS PROMPTLY.

Sometimes new frontline leaders find it hard to point out unacceptable behaviors. You have just been promoted to manage the people who were your peers and even friends just a couple of days ago. It can feel awkward to communicate with them now as their leader. Even worse, you may have to correct your crew on shortcuts they saw you take last week.

One way to approach this is to say, "I know how easy it is to take this shortcut. Now that I'm responsible for your safety, I realize how important it is to your safety to do it the right way rather than the quick way." No amount of time or cost savings can make up for a fatality or life-changing injury.

As you make suggestions for safety improvements, build on the positive and minimize the negative. I am not suggesting there is no room for discipline. In fact, if you don't insist that expectations be met and then fail to follow through when those expectations fail to materialize, you will have no creditability with your team. I'm suggesting you do everything you can to build up your crew instead of tearing them down. When there's an issue, instead of reprimanding employees, seek a creative moment. Ask your team for suggestions on improvements. What can we do differently? How can we learn from other crews' experience with this type of hazard? Encourage everyone to look for and rectify potentially hazardous situations. Encourage a culture where people say, "Oh man, I didn't think about that! Now that I know it happened, I can understand how I've got to watch for it, or it could happen to me."

Put people in the correct classification. One of the easiest ways to correct unsafe or unhealthy acts promptly is to prevent them. You can do this by making sure you place people in the correct classification for their skillset, beginning with a proper assessment. In our industry, where there is significant turnover, putting people in the proper classification is hard. Once we realize people are incorrectly classified, we now have an urgent safety issue to address immediately. Think of the risk associated with an apprentice's assumption of the role they have been working toward. Is the new electrician confident? Does today's doctor know more than yesterday's resident? Can the new line technician feel comfortable asking questions? A promotion should not mean an end to questions and guidance.

Engage employees to participate in safety. Integrate safety into everything you do. Encourage your team to watch for unsafe acts and high-risk behaviors. Always give honest feedback in the most positive way possible. Create a microculture of safety that encourages team members to speak up, even if it means revealing their own poor judgment. You can do this by involving employees, answering questions honestly, asking for opinions, and managing the negatives. Train and develop employees continually. Make sure they understand what they know and what they might not know. Explain that what we don't know often turns into an incident.

As a leader, you may need to call somebody out on their actions, but it doesn't always need to be negative. Call out good things whenever possible so that correcting negative habits becomes part of routine feedback. Behavior modification can be more successful with balanced input than it is with nothing but negative feedback.

4. LEARN TO COMMUNICATE EFFECTIVELY.

As a new frontline leader, this may be the first time your job focuses on communication rather than action. Now is the opportunity to use your technical expertise and experience to connect and engage with others. Like electrical work, effective communication requires planning and preparation. Listen carefully and avoid interrupting. Think before you speak. Show empathy. Make all communication intentional and direct.

Remember, what you don't say says a lot about you. If you're in a hurry to finish a job and you overlook the shortcut your crew just took in the name of time, what does your crew see? Is your silence an endorsement? Is there now a new standard operating procedure invoked when it's convenient? Your crew may now wonder what else can be compromised in the name of time or speed.

Most importantly, be clear, be consistent, and be kind. You will earn the respect of your crew, peers, and supervisors. Everyone welcomes predictable expectations and leaders who use their experience to lift others.

Set clear expectations. Regulations and policies that may be obvious to you can be a challenge for people on your team. One region manager I know has simple directives for most things. For example, he says to all new employees, "Don't climb higher than four feet high or enter a hole greater than three feet deep without seeking guidance first." This advice is clear because it's simple, and it illustrates a visual reference for anyone, even a person who has never worked in the construction industry. Be sure to point out hazards to new employees; some new employees may not realize a wire on the ground is still hot, and we don't want them to reach down and touch it.

Investigate all injuries, illnesses, and property damage incidents. We assume everyone knows early detection mitigates risk. Watch for unsafe acts and stop the behavior quickly before somebody gets in trouble or the new action becomes standard operating procedure. Bad practices lead to inconsistent and hazardous results. Small, unchecked incidents increase risk.

Some people may suggest that digging into the minor issues takes away from more significant major problems. A key to creating a No Compromise Safety Culture is continually looking for more innovative ways to do our work. We understand that even the most minor event is worth investigating—not to punish—but to learn. This doesn't mean we should spend excessive time on something small. We always strive for excellence, and part of that process is understanding why we didn't get the desired result. A No Compromise Safety Culture doesn't guarantee zero incidents; what it does guarantee is promoting the lowest risk environment possible.

5. LEARN TO LEAD OTHERS.

When you're in a leadership role, the shadow you cast is enormous. I don't care what anybody says about your job title, the amount of financial responsibility you have, or the number of people you manage. If your role has an impact on people, your value must always be safety.

Often, we mistakenly assume leadership styles are intuitive. This is simply not true. Leadership style, like many other skills, is a learned behavior. A well-known and influential leadership style, servant leadership, is a great model for frontline leaders. Servant leadership calls for the leader to focus on cultivating people rather than focusing on profits. When people rise in success, profits rise as well. This philosophy mirrors a No Compromise Safety Culture in that we also focus on developing people who can cultivate the lowest risk environment possible.

Some of the guidelines of servant leadership you can adopt immediately are to lead by example, clearly communicate expectations and instructions, and observe and enforce rules and procedures. You can address shortcomings through coaching when expectations are not being met, treat others as you wish to be treated, and be patient when you teach and explain the same thing repeatedly. As you might expect, the skills associated with servant leadership are patience, kindness, humility, respectfulness, selflessness, forgiveness, honesty, and commitment.

6. UNDERSTAND THAT YOU ARE RESPONSIBLE AND ACCOUNTABLE FOR YOUR EMPLOYEES' ACTIONS.

Frontline leaders are only as good as how their crew performs when they are away. Ask any supervisor, "If an employee has an incident on your day off, is it your fault?" Many may say no because another person is acting as the crew supervisor that day. In fact, the answer is yes, you are responsible for your crew's actions on the job even when you are away.

Some people may be surprised to learn that the National Electrical Safety Code manual mandates the frontline leader is held legally responsible for the people who report to them. Employees must perform in the safest manner at all times regardless of whether you are present or not. Your daily leadership and coaching should guide their behavior even when you are not present. It's a bit like parenting—we expect our children to be on their best behavior when we are not around. We hold them accountable when they do not meet our expectations because we know that is key to successful parenting.

The most important job you have as a supervisor is to keep your employees safe. As you coach and demonstrate clear and easy-to-follow safe practices, you develop a culture within your crew. We want them to perform safely because they recognize the value in it, not because we're watching.

Make working safely a condition of employment. If you have an employee who is willing to put themselves and others at risk, you make the hard call: "I'm not willing to let you get hurt on the job, so you no longer need to be in this job." Remain firm with high expectations while addressing problems and reinforcing positive behaviors swiftly and consistently.

Own your work zone. You are responsible for your work zone, including all the people, procedures, materials, and equipment in it. You own both the "be prepared" and "confident" in this role. Be ready to handle a management visit to the job site. When a senior leader or other guest visits your work zone, you determine if that person is allowed to enter the work zone. You make sure that person is safe by wearing proper personal protective equipment (PPE) and following all safety protocols and that they're escorted from the moment they step into your area. Manage your work zone and pay attention to what you own.

Be 100% sure you know what you're doing *before* you do it! When we say, "Know that you know what you're doing," we mean two things: Be confident in *what* you know and be willing to admit *when* you don't know.

First, be confident in what you know. Part of doing a great job in anything, especially safety, is having confidence in your work. I can tell you all day long that you know what you're doing; the important thing is for *you* to know that you know what you're doing. The best way to gain confidence in your work is to take ownership of it. You own all of it, the successes and the failures. Confidence in leading means you dare to identify mistakes—including your own—make the right decisions and corrections, and move forward.

Second, be willing to admit when you don't know something. No one will expect you to know everything you need to know to be an outstanding frontline leader on your first day in the role. This approach is essential to establishing your credibility. Your team will know when you're confident and when you're winging it. By having the courage to ask questions, your team will know you are open to feedback and that they, too, can ask questions.

In the excitement of a new role, we may feel embarrassed to admit that we don't know everything. Our self-imposed pressure to succeed makes us want to say yes to everything. Though it may feel counterintuitive, it's a sign of great strength to say no when you are uncertain. In our industry, we cannot allow a leader to put anyone in harm's way without making sure they understand how to do a task without injury. Understand the ramifications of your situation before you make decisions. Your training and experience will tell you what is safe and unsafe. Stick with it. Be confident in your decisions. Only approve things you can do with 100% confidence in safety. You want your actions always to say, "I value safety."

7. ENSURE PROPERLY TRAINED EMPLOYEES FOLLOW POLICIES AND PROCEDURES.

We often think training is the answer to any operational weakness. This is not true. There are people trained to drive safely who still put themselves in harm's way by speeding. Knowing how to do something safely is not enough to prevent incidents. As the frontline leader, it's your responsibility to make sure your crew not only knows *how* to do things safely but is *motivated* to do things safely. People development is an integral part of your job, and the most influential leaders are often the best trainers. Employees need to feel they have the freedom to demand safe work conditions, prevent hazards, correct deficiencies on the job, and stop unsafe work. They must remain steadfast in their safe work practices, even under stressful circumstances.

They also need to understand we do not use safety as an excuse to get out of work. One of the best ways to ensure your team's safety is to make sure they understand *how* to be safe. In addition to properly training employees, you must follow-up to make sure they utilize the training in everything they do. Use your organization's policies and procedures as tools to make your points and train on the job every day.

Know your audience and relate to them individually.

Understand that, as a frontline leader, you are dealing with all kinds of people. Everyone on the crew will bring varying levels of knowledge and experience, attitudes, and beliefs. They will learn in different ways. You need to adapt your conversations and training style to each person. Meet them where they are. As adult learners, we take new information and assimilate it into what we already know. For example, someone who comes from a family of line technicians may already know the lingo. Someone who has worked in the industry for several years will understand how to complete many tasks without detailed instructions. You can figure out what people already know by simply asking them, "What do you know about X?" Avoid questions that can be answered with "yes" or "no." If you ask most new employees, "Do you know how to do this task?" they will automatically say "yes," even if they can't do it with 100% proficiency because they want to prove their value.

Some people learn by hearing things while others need to witness a process to comprehend it. To meet the needs of both learners, you'll need to say and show them what you mean.

You will also have employees from different generations who may learn in different ways. Let's say you have an older, more seasoned person on your crew. This person may have just purchased an iPhone and asked their grandchildren to set up apps for them. You may also have a younger person on your crew who recently graduated from school and can find information on the internet in a matter of seconds. Consider how each of these people processes information—old school versus new school. Marry the two and use their differences to your advantage. Pull each person into the conversation to compare notes and help you build a team that collaborates and performs at a higher level.

There is no "safety training," only training that includes safety. Training is an ongoing process. It doesn't occur solely in the classroom. People—no matter what industry they work in—will say that they learned more on the job than in their formal education. Experiential learning is good news for you because you can seek and implement teachable moments every day instead of creating and executing formal training. Look for opportunities to teach and mentor. What weakness in your process seems to be popping up frequently? What do new employees need to know before they begin work on your crew? How can crew members mentor each other? Seeing training as an ongoing process not only makes it easier to implement but also makes training more effective.

For many frontline leaders, accountability for crew training and development is a new responsibility. Understand that your goal as a leader is to grow people into their next role. We often refer to this as "next person up," meaning we continually prepare everyone in the organization for a more significant position or promotion. We do this in three steps. First, we learn it. This is when you train and coach people to do their current job. Second, we do it. This step is when you begin to groom people for their next role. Third, we teach it. This step is when your employees train the next generation to take over their own job.

Personal development. In addition to grooming people on your team, you will need to grow into your current role and develop into your next position by educating yourself on safety. Between OSHA and other governing bodies, there are hundreds of directives for the frontline leader to consume and implement. As the frontline leader, you are responsible for teaching your team governing regulations and in-house policies and procedures, as well as documenting this process for your organization. An integral part of this process is figuring out why it's essential to do things a certain way and explaining to employees how it relates to them. Look to your peers and supervisor for help in coaching and managing your team. Learn how to prioritize projects and goals, identify areas of weakness, and understand the best ways to adapt to your behavior in the new role.

8. DEAL WITH CONFLICT.

Conflict is inevitable; there is no way around it, and you don't want to discourage it outright. How you deal with it influences more than just today's decisions; it shapes the culture of your team now and in the future. When conflict happens, leaders generally respond in one of three ways. First, they may become blindly submissive to other people's ideas. These leaders feel uncomfortable around conflict, so they avoid it. When the leader doesn't step up with a solution, members of a group can create even more competition as they jockey to promote their opinions. Don't be wishy-washy with your decisions. It can cause you to lose the respect of your team. When you are receptive to your team's suggestions, you will gain their respect.

Secondly, some leaders welcome conflict and use it to promote dictatorial leadership. They usually resolve conflict with one-sided answers, which leads to poor decision-making and low morale.

Lastly, some leaders use conflict in a positive manner to teach, learn, and grow their teams. This style generates the most effective outcomes. Leaders listen carefully without making judgments, and they encourage team members at all levels to contribute. They understand conflict can highlight weaknesses and give us a chance to make valuable corrections. They see conflict as an opportunity to develop people by teaching them to think about things differently.

Whenever you end up in a conflict situation, think about something important in your value system and personality for which you have a strong opinion. Then think about how you would feel if somebody tried to challenge you on that subject. It would be tough to change your opinion. Often, we hold onto beliefs and habits with such determination we cannot see any faults. At work, we feel the need to defend our opinions as if we are protecting our honor. You may think, "I know I'm right. Why doesn't this person see things the way I do?" Do your career and your relationships a favor by loosening that grip on your opinions. Be open to new ways of thinking and working, and you'll be amazed to see the opportunities opening up for you.

9. MAKE IT STICK WITH RELENTLESS REPETITION.

Permanent change is hard when we've spent years reinforcing a bad habit. You can't just say it one time and go on. If something needs to be corrected, fix it and train everyone using various examples. You must be *smart* positive. Everything you do has to be intentional and implemented with intelligent, positive reinforcement. You probably already know that most people typically need to hear about it seven times before it sticks. For a new behavior to become a habit, people need to do it for greater than thirty days. It can be eye-opening for crews to hear what frontline leaders have experienced, whether it's good or bad. Look for the most positive way to fix a negative and make it a daily habit through relentless repetition.

Summary of Safety Truth #4: As goes the frontline leader, so goes safety.

We can strive to have everything perfect in the organization. We can have supportive leadership, targeted recruitment, and excellent training, but no amount of external work or effort will change the impact of a weak frontline leader. To achieve a No Compromise Safety Culture, the frontline leader must lead and own safety in the work zone. Each person above and below the frontline leader should see the frontline leader as integral to the support they need to excel in their own role. Frontline leaders must translate safe work methods into positive behaviors, habits, and ultimately a No Compromise Safety Culture.

Professionalism drives positive safety performance.

Safety is a professional skill set. When we view ourselves as professionals in our field, our performance automatically rises to a higher level.

Positive safety performance is not magic or a jinx.

Once my organization began to see significant and positive results from the No Compromise Safety Culture approach to work, I delightfully shared the news throughout every division, both high and low. At a meeting with an operational unit, I praised everyone for completing the last quarter without an incident. Everyone clapped and patted themselves on the back for a job well done.

Afterward, a colleague came up to me and said, "Why did you bring up our no-incident rate at the meeting? You're going to jinx us."

"Positive safety performance is not magic or a jinx. Everyone worked hard to accomplish it," I told him. "We need to acknowledge their success, praise everyone for getting us there, and identify how to do it again next quarter." The next step, I explained, is to keep our guard up even though we met our goal. Positive safety performance is an ongoing objective. We must always approach it one task at a time by focusing on the work at hand.

The question that followed me around the rest of the day was this: Of all the occupations in the world, why do transmission and distribution line technicians see positive safety performance as magic or a jinx instead of seeing ourselves as finely trained, vetted professionals? We are deliberate in everything we do and possess a hard-earned, finely-tuned skillset.

There may be several reasons for this way of thinking. Traditionally, our industry attracts people who are not afraid to take risks; working at heights with high voltage under extreme conditions does not scare us. In the past, we viewed ourselves with a cowboy mentality rather than with a professional mentality. We arrive immediately after the hurricane or tornado has cleared the area to put hospitals, senior housing, and sick kids back on power. We can climb a 40-foot utility pole in a matter of seconds and even compete to see who can climb the pole the fastest in events we call rodeos. We're tough. We aren't scared to do technical work on steel transmission structures rising to 200 feet. We work in all weather conditions—three-digit temperatures, freezing rain, bitter cold, and high winds—because our customers count on us to restore electricity in bad weather. We're proud to be the heroes who show up during ice storms so people can get their lives back to normal.

And it takes time, commitment, and years of training to advance from apprentice to line technician. This trade can't be learned by trial and error. We need to recognize we are highly skilled professionals with hard-earned technical expertise. We don't just run around climbing poles and playing with high voltage electricity. We go through rigorous education, training, and apprenticeship programs. Our work requires specific, calculated steps that demand we think, plan, execute, and follow-up with the same precision as a surgeon. If something goes wrong, we handle it in the precise manner explained in our standard operating procedures.

We line technicians need to raise our standards to match our skills, and safety is one of those skills. Consider this comparison. Let's say you need an operation. You expect everyone—from the nurse who prepares you for surgery and the anesthesiologist who puts you to sleep to the surgeon who performs the procedure—to approach your treatment in the most appropriate, specific way that ensures the best outcome with the least amount of risk. You trust that when they are caring for you, they will focus only on you and the job they are performing at that moment. How would you feel if, right before your surgery, your doctor said to the surgical team, "Don't talk about the great results we've had so far today. You might jinx us." Does that even make sense? Medicine is not based on luck; it is based on science and proficiency. We regard medical professionals as experts, and we respect their opinions and their work. We assume they consistently perform at the highest level of safety and protocols, and we know their success depends on education, training, experience, and precision, not magic or a jinx. Our professional skills earn the same respect.

Safety is a professional skill set.

We operate in a high-risk industry with elevated consequences. Nearly every professional in transmission and distribution knows about someone who was severely injured or killed doing electrical work. Occasionally, when one survives a consequential incident, the story becomes a badge of honor. "Did you see the burn marks on their hand? I heard they picked up an unknown hot wire and had extensive entry and exit wounds." To be great at your job—even revered—your goal should not be to survive a near-miss but to create the lowest risk environment possible. We nurture this environment with a professional skill set that begins with safety.

Manage with a positive bias.

Humans are hardwired toward negativity. Research suggests remembering adverse events allowed humans to survive; we focused on bad outcomes as a way of avoiding them in the future. That's why the news that often grabs our attention is negative, horrific, or sensational. In transmission and distribution, it's easy to identify what went wrong after we observe risky behavior or near misses. Mistakes are easy to spot with 20/20 hindsight.

It is also human nature to overlook the things that are going well. A person can do nineteen steps in a task perfectly but miss number twenty. What do we remember?

Number twenty. Acknowledging only mistakes is deflating. Over time, framing feedback in the most positive way can may it comfortable to bring up problems. It can encourage the person listening to be more receptive because they sense value for what they do well 99% of the time. It can generate a cultural shift that promotes excellence and leads to positive safety performance.

Let's say you are now a safety director. You visit a job site to observe the implementation of your organization's safety program in the field. When you arrive, you see a line technician working high voltage with perfect precision, and you are impressed until that same person throws something from the bucket to the ground.

When you get ready to close out your site visit, your only feedback is, "You shouldn't have thrown something from the bucket to the ground. Somebody could have gotten hurt." If you approach safety in this manner, you miss the opportunity to recognize all the positives this person worked so hard to do to be safe working in high voltage. After you leave, they say, "Are you kidding me? Is that all he could find? Did he come here just to find something wrong?"

Use feedback to inspire, motivate, and reinforce behaviors.

I discovered that positive reinforcement, when appropriate, is far more impactful than criticism. A crew may have just completed a complex job without a hitch. This same crew may have left tools and materials on the ground. If you focus on the tools on the ground rather than the complex job, you defeat the purpose of feedback. Feedback should inspire people to change behaviors, and inspiration comes from finding the positive in a situation. Always highlight the good things first. Choose your words carefully to be more of a coach than critic. Use non-inflammatory language such as "I observe this happening" instead of "you always do this."

I'm not suggesting you ignore the small things like dropping tools from a lowered bucket. You can't just shut your eyes and blindly be positive. Rather, focus on the success of the crew. They completed a high-quality job while working to create the lowest risk environment possible. You *should* discuss unacceptable behaviors as long as you do so constructively. Actual behavioral change takes genuine, appropriate positive reinforcement. Positive reinforcement is not manipulating people, and it is not trying to keep people from doing something or trick them into doing a specific behavior. It is simply the basic fact that we all prefer to hear what we did well. The more positive reinforcement we give to celebrate our teams' successes, the more likely leaders will influence true behavioral change.

You can learn a lot about people by looking at their trucks.

One of the best ways to understand an organization's culture is to notice the little things, like the housekeeping you see inside and outside of workers' trucks. Notice whether the vehicle is neat and tidy. It doesn't have to be pristine—after all, we are construction workers—but it should be orderly. Things are put away in the right place. There are no extra scraps left lying around the cab, and there are no sharp ends exposed. Tidiness is an indication someone thinks about their work from start to finish, and it reflects how that individual will go about doing the entire job.

Even though this little habit may not seem like an essential part of a worker's job, it is fundamental because we want our trucks to look good to our customers and in our communities. It shows a sense of pride in our profession and ownership in our company. Our trucks are mobile billboards moving through counties and states advertising our company as a competent and well-run organization. Every part of our work—from our physical appearance to our trucks and job sites—represents how we do business. Thoughtful attention to detail is a foundation for safety, and that's a win for employees, stakeholders, directors, and customers.

Don't cut off the end of the ham until you know why you are doing it.

Do you remember your first day of algebra class? My teacher went over equations the entire period. She talked about the order of operations and advised us to do the same thing on both sides of the equal sign. She said we needed to get "X" by itself but never told us why. For adults, understanding *why* we do something is as important as understanding *what* we are doing.

Here's why getting to why is vital. It's Thanksgiving. A couple is in the kitchen prepping food for the holiday dinner. The wife starts cutting off the end of a ham, and the husband says, "Why are you cutting off the end of the ham?" She says, "Hmmm. I don't know. It's what my mother always did."

She calls her mother to ask, "Why do we always cut off the end of a ham?" Her mother says, "It's what my mother always did. I'll call your grandmother and ask her." The mother calls the grandmother and asks, "Why did you always cut off the end of the ham?" to which her grandmother replies, "I never had a pan big enough to cook the whole ham."

Understanding the why is an essential part of learning, particularly for new employees. People are more apt to follow established procedures when they understand the end goal. You can coach them by explaining, "Here's why we do this task this way," or "Here's how this process helps you to be efficient and safe."

Imagine you're at a job briefing, and you have a new crew member who just graduated from high school. You give one of the most brilliant job briefings you've ever given, and you turn to that young person and say, "Did you understand all of that?" They nod and quietly say, "Uh-huh," even though they don't have a clue about what you just said. That new employee will need to learn every tiny detail from the bottom up, and explaining why we do a task is crucial to adult learning strategy. When we place new information into context, it helps others understand and apply it later.

Open communication is key.

As a leader, creating an atmosphere of open communication is not difficult. It starts with respect. Everyone on your crew should feel comfortable questioning each other, and everyone needs to accept questions with grace and humility. In a well-managed organization, employees show mutual respect by communicating in a respectful, nonpersonal way. For example, when they bring up an issue, they choose the right moment, which may be out of earshot of the rest of the crew. They use the word "I" instead of "you" when making observations, so the other person is less defensive. They're not scared to tell you what they believe in or if they think a task should be done differently. Most importantly, as the leader in the crew, you set the tone for this kind of behavior. Employees learn the importance of respect from you and how you interact with each person on your team.

Open communication is not always about saying how great things are going. We should be able to communicate a near miss, ask a question, make a comment, or say we don't understand something without feeling embarrassed. We must remove the fear of retaliation, ridicule, or shame and hone our ability to communicate as a professional tool for improving our work. We should also disagree with someone and have a professional conversation about our opinions without conflict. Debates and disagreements are not hostile if handled positively. Each person should be open to hearing other ideas, even if they still disagree after listening. Resolving conflict through open communication can move us forward in our safety culture. No Compromise is about sharing experiences and opinions, learning from each other, and bringing people together to discuss operating more efficiently and safely.

Be each other's keeper.

In our industry, people often refer to looking out for each other as "being each other's keeper." We take care of our own with great pride. Crews pool their resources to help a colleague in need. We may gently tease each other, but we protect one another when it comes down to business. This family-oriented tradition helps build a positive culture. It's also a great way to lay the foundation for a No Compromise Safety Culture.

In safety, when we look after each other, our entire perspective changes. We are willing to challenge each other using a caring attitude. We are receptive to suggestions because we trust the teammate has our best interest in mind. When an entire crew operates with this mentality, the whole team takes on the knowledge base of sometimes decades of collaborative skill and experience. Morale improves as confidence goes up because we know what we're doing. We work together. We look out for each other.

Many years ago, when I was a line technician, I experienced a moment when someone was my keeper. I remember that day clearly; it was the spark that lit the fire of the importance of being each other's keeper as the foundation of a low-risk environment. Another technician and I were working in separate buckets on the same pole. We were repairing a broken cross arm, which was a two-person job that required cover-up. My colleague in the other bucket had about thirty more years of experience than I did. He was a crusty, no-nonsense veteran lineman. He wasn't inclined to chit-chat; he was all business. We discussed the job beforehand, but he didn't try to tell me how to do it.

Right after we finished securing the proper cover, he looked up and quietly and calmly said, "Sheridan, stop. Turn around real easy and look behind you. I think you need to add another hose." I slowly turned around and saw that he was making a great suggestion. I added the extra cover, and we went about our work. At the time, I appreciated his tip. He may have seemed crusty and old to me, but I realized he wasn't going to let me get hurt on the job. He was intentionally calm; following his advice significantly lowered the risk associated with the situation.

As I progressed into various safety roles, I understood that this line technician's quiet demeanor and sage advice were the epitome of a No Compromise Safety Culture.

Take your time. Do your work in a methodical, calculated way. Look beyond your task. Watch out for your colleagues. Be each other's keeper.

This day proved critical in my career. As I progressed into various safety roles throughout the years, I understood this line technician's quiet demeanor and sage advice were synonymous with a No Compromise Safety Culture. Through his example, he taught me that rules, measurements, and data made up only three-quarters of our job; the remaining quarter encompassed making sure no one suffered an injury. I took my time and did my work in a systematic, calculated way. I looked beyond my task to look out for my colleagues. I became their keeper.

Do sweat the small stuff.

When I visit job sites and talk with crews about safety, I actively look for clues that indicate if the team has a positive, thriving safety culture. One of my challenges as a safety leader is maintaining a positive presence without ignoring small, negative behaviors. A meaningful way to achieve and sustain a No Compromise Safety Culture is to sweat the small stuff.

People often ask me why I'm so concerned about fixing outwardly small, negative behaviors. They ask, "Sheridan, why are you so worried about the small stuff?" To me, small behaviors indicate a more committed attitude toward safety. For example, *not* using a turn signal when you drive tells me you are not concerned about the safety of your passengers, other drivers, and pedestrians. Your turn signal is the way you communicate what you intend to do. It's true that not using a signal to indicate a turn probably doesn't compromise safety as much as driving ten miles over the speed limit might, but it's still a critical part of driving safely. What if you hit a pedestrian crossing the street who assumed you were not turning because you didn't use a signal? It would be devastating to hurt someone over something as simple as a directional.

On a larger scale, ostensibly insignificant poor habits can suggest more prominent, harmful behaviors that could be far more dangerous. We must sweat the small stuff because it's often a precursor to the big stuff. A person who doesn't value the use of turn signals may also compromise other safety protocols. No matter the task at hand, the intelligent way to do it is to use the safest possible procedure; relentless repetition of the correct technique becomes second nature. We develop muscle memory similar to what we learn in sports. If you repeatedly swing a golf club the wrong way, it becomes a hard habit to break.

In the turn signal example, what is your responsibility if you witness the driver violating safe driving practices? In a No Compromise Safety Culture, the role of the teammate is equally essential. If you are riding with someone who breaks the law by not using a turn signal, and you don't say anything, are you potentially liable for a resulting incident? In safety, when you fail to mention a violation, your silence *condones* that behavior, and it soon becomes the standard operating procedure for you both.

To break the cycle, you will need to judge how to broach the subject. You might respectfully mention turn signals are an integral part of being a safe driver. You can ask the person to use a signal and perhaps give the person an example of an incident that resulted from no-signal driving. You could even simply say, "Hey, I get nervous when you don't use a blinker. I want to make sure you're driving safely, even when I'm not in the truck." Every safety-conscious person must be aware staying silent about a negative safety behavior is an endorsement of that behavior.

Another small but potentially dangerous act is not putting wheel chocks on a parked vehicle. Each and every line technician knows it's standard operating procedure to chock a truck's wheels, so why do so many skip this critical parking step? How much time and effort does it take to accomplish this simple but necessary step? If we can prevent catastrophic injuries such as rolling back and hitting someone or rolling back while a crew member works from a raised bucket, why is this ever an issue? Therein lies the problem; people don't see this small step as necessary. If we don't view something as required, we are less likely to do it.

Lead through safety.

A fundamental obligation of any professional is to lead. In safety, this obligation means everything you do creates the lowest risk environment possible. Safety should be the number one concern from the pre-job briefing to the end-of-day closeout. We must follow every law, policy, and procedure every time. There will be times when it may be tempting to skip steps on certain tasks. You may think, "I've done this dozens of times. This shortcut won't hurt." While it is okay to be confident in your work, it's never okay to be cocky, skip a standard operating procedure, and create a high-risk environment that could lead to an injury for you or others.

Let's say a crew is replacing a pole and needs to transfer a conductor. Standard operating procedure calls for two hoists to manage this task safely. The crew leader falls into the trap of thinking, "We don't need two hoists. We can easily do this with one hoist to save time." Because of the angle and use of only one hoist, the slack created causes an energized wire to hit a grounded wire, producing a phase-to-ground contact and an unintended outage but no injuries. Everyone is relieved no one was hurt, but we still have consequences, including interrupted service to our customers. How will a power outage, even a short one, affect them? What if one of those customers is a medical facility, and their backup power source is inoperable? What if a person needs an oxygen machine to breathe? What could happen if we interrupt power to traffic signals at a major intersection? We must always show respect for our customers and our community.

If only one hoist were necessary to complete this task, that would be the standard operating procedure. During the root cause analysis investigation of this incident, someone asks the crew leader, "During this task, did you wear hard hats, safety glasses, flame resistant clothing, and fall protection?" The crew leader answers yes to every question. Then the investigation team asks, "Did you use two hoists?"

"No. I thought we could do it with just one," shows the incorrect choice to follow some protocols but not all. Using two hoists is just as important as the other protocols. PPE is always the last measure we take for safety. Standard operating procedure, such as using two hoists instead of one, is the first measure.

How can we get everyone to follow this protocol with the same commitment to wearing hard hats and other PPE? Our crews should see safety as imperative, not an inconvenience. In a No Compromise Safety Culture, everyone thinks, "Isn't it great to work for a company that values safety so much that they provide and require the safest possible tools and methods?"

Equally important is the investigation into how the deviation from policy occurred to prevent the same mistake from happening again. Contrary to popular belief, a post-incident investigation is not a witch hunt; it is an opportunity to identify the root cause. Did this drift away from standard operating procedures occur over time, or was it an isolated decision? What is it about this particular crew that allowed this deviation? Was the decision to deviate blatant disregard or motivated by deadlines? Is this drift happening with other teams and with other standard operating procedures? Where did this task turn from a safe operation to an unsafe one? How was risk managed before and during this task? A quick assessment across the company might identify whether this behavior is systemic or singular.

You cannot use safety to justify operational wants over needs or as an excuse.

When organizations begin to integrate safety, some employees try to use safety as an excuse. They justify requests for new equipment, ask for more employees on a job, and stop work in the name of safety. My question for them is, "Are you breaking safety rules?" They answer, "Of course not!" Then how will purchasing a new piece of equipment, adding employees, and stopping work change the situation? You cannot allow all challenges to become a safety issue. Safety is a tool to be used as an enabling factor to get a job done, not a hindrance to productivity.

Employees in all industries delight in new equipment purchases: new iPads, new vehicles, and new PPE. In transmission and distribution, procurement often receives requests for new bucket trucks because employees cannot safely climb utility poles. This is not a safety issue. It doesn't matter if you have a bucket truck for utility pole work or not. What matters is that you are qualified to work safely from a bucket or a pole. If you cannot work from a pole, human resources need to revisit your classification and ensure you are competent to do the work detailed in your job description. Frontline supervisors need to plan each job so that all tasks are performed by trained and fully qualified individuals. An unqualified line technician is a safety hazard; putting them in a bucket will not solve this problem.

Another comment we sometimes hear from workers is that they need more staffing for a "safe operation." For example, they have five employees to complete their task, and they suggest eight people would be more appropriate. The real question is, does having only five people cause them to do unsafe acts or procedures, or are they motivated by some other factor, such as speed or physical endurance? While the number of workers on a job may change efficiencies, safety should never depend on how many people are on the job. If we look at safety as a professional skill set, the number of workers on a job shouldn't affect safe behaviors. The work you are doing is not a safety issue until you break a safety rule. If you follow protocol, tasks are completed as expected.

Use safety to do the work, not to get out of work.

Employees should feel comfortable making suggestions and requests concerning operations and efficiency. Employees should be free to say they don't know how to do a particular task or stop unsafe work without fear of retaliation. They not only have the right to halt hazardous work, but they also have an obligation to stop unsafe work. Technicians should be assigned to tasks they are fully qualified to take on and none other. If you don't know how to perform a function, you need to advise your supervisor.

One CEO I know says, "I want everybody in this company to know they can say 'no' to unsafe work." This bold statement requires an exemplary level of trust between the CEO and the employees. Employees trust the company to provide the means to achieve the lowest risk work environment possible. The CEO trusts employees to perform in the safest manner and advise the chain of command about unsafe work. This mutual trust means we cannot use safety as an excuse when it has nothing to do with the request. Such excuses would be an abuse of power and would weaken the safety culture.

Achieve positive safety performance by creating the lowest risk environment possible.

We must take all voiced safety concerns seriously with a commitment to resolve them promptly. The only way to do this effectively is for everyone to understand there is no way to remove 100% of all risk from any situation. The goal is to create the lowest risk work environment possible. We focus on the task, anticipate the challenges ahead of time, and control hazards. Part of our commitment to each other is creating a low-risk environment, no matter where you are working or what task you are performing.

The reality is that no company or organization can conceivably have a detailed safety procedure for everything. For example, we don't have a protocol for getting in and out of a truck. We count on you to use your training and sound judgment to do that safely. As a transmission and distribution professional, you should be able to recognize and control the hazards. In the absence of a written procedure, your job is to know how to create a low-risk environment. As you progress in your experience and safety journey, it will be easier to manage the lowest risk environment.

Summary of Safety Truth #5: Professionalism drives positive safety performance.

In our industry, we can never entirely eliminate risk. We define an acceptable level of risk, and we never exceed that. Standard operating procedures exist to reduce risk to an acceptable level through specialized, professional training and job classifications. We must never compromise these procedures through a misguided desire to complete a task more quickly. We need to see ourselves as highly skilled professionals who use standard operating procedures to reduce risk for our crewmates, communities, and ourselves. Though safety is one of those values where it is easy to make your points by highlighting the negative, our goal in a No Compromise culture is to demonstrate and promote safety with positive reinforcement with a professional attitude and performance throughout all we do.

Pay attention to what is going on in your organization.

Organizational leaders must understand how daily, sometimes casual, decisions and the actions of individual employees can affect safety. Upper management, safety professionals, and field leaders must follow internal safety performance trends with the same enthusiasm applied to business trends.

It can be hard to create and sustain positive safety performance. Transmission and distribution is complex work with wide-ranging variables that make it hard to measure safety. In our world, where minor incidents can have significant consequences, we must put serious effort into safety performance. There isn't one singular practice applicable across industries; what works for one organization or division may not work for another. Thanks to thousands of pages of regulated safety policies and procedures for our industry, we know what steps to take to complete a task safely. Knowing what to do isn't the issue; the issue is that we need to *manage* safety actively. We need to dig in and understand what is happening in the organization that may unintentionally compromise safety.

What you pay attention to gets attention.

We need to pay attention to where we focus our attention. An SVP of operations once told me, "When I'm in a disaster or high-pressure situation, I'll catch myself thinking,

'We've got to get this done.' A customer can have a legitimate need to get the power back on, and we've got to set that pole."

This mentality, though well-intentioned, can push us to take more risk than is necessary. We are in a trade where only a select few have the aptitude and training to do this job. We want to ride in, fix the pole quickly, and move on to the next to get the lights back on for as many customers as possible. It can be too easy to adopt a get-it-done mentality in the name of speed and urgency, but that is where the potential for injury lies. Don't get too cocky to get the job done and let the weight of the responsibility force you to take unnecessary risks. Our cowboy swagger comes from a sense of responsibility, pride, and a natural inclination to meet the customer's needs. These are good feelings for all the right reasons as long as you don't jeopardize your own safety.

A senior leader I know decided to spend 25% of their time in the field observing safety management firsthand. At every job site this leader visited, the managers set them up to meet with the highest performers. They wanted the senior leader to see only the parts of the business where crews focused on safety. The senior leader would spend time with these top performers at each site, asking them how things were going and what management could do to help them work more safely.

The leader was not fooled. He said to the managers, "I've spoken with the people who lead in safety. Now I want to hear from the people who are not as developed. I want to hear from everyone on the crew."

The leader spent a full day at each site, giving him ample time to see and hear field operations. For each new group, the first few minutes were awkward and guarded. The crew felt cautious about what they should and should not reveal. By the end of the visit, though, the crews shared concerns, success stories, and challenges. They grew comfortable with this leader because he assured them he intended to gather safety information and connect with employees. Their well-being was his primary purpose.

These visits spurred many positive safety behaviors and actions. While planning for the upcoming visit, one frontline leader told the crew, "Everybody knows we don't have two different ways of working. We don't change our methods just because someone is watching. We have one way of doing it, and that's the safe way. Don't let this visitor distract you from doing your work safely." For frontline and crew leaders, having the senior leader visit their site validated their methods and practices. They demonstrated to the senior leader their deliberate commitment to safe operations through adherence to safety protocols like wearing proper PPE and maneuvering through a job site safely. They spoke frankly about their safety challenges.

As a result, the field crews saw the senior leader's visit as supportive. They asked questions about the business and his background. If the leader lacked experience in transmission and distribution, the crew took the time to explain the technical parts of the job. Crew members valued the opportunity to share opinions and concerns directly with the top of the organization. They saw the senior leader listening to their concerns and witnessing their successes. In turn, the field crew learned about the goals and challenges of upper management and gained a 360-degree perspective of the company as a whole. This caring senior leader built trust by demonstrating honesty, integrity, and genuine concern, all of which are building blocks in a No Compromise Safety Culture.

When a leader steps into the field, they have an opportunity to accomplish so many things. In addition to gaining a better understanding of the workings of the crews and the challenges of the job, they see firsthand the implementation of the company's safety culture. They observe how crew leaders handle interruptions and visitors. They listen to crew members describe the challenges of operating safely and hear employees talk about their work with pride. They think differently about how future decisions impact those doing the work.

The leader also starts a ripple effect through the company. At a staff meeting, they may share new knowledge that helps procurement or human resources consider a different perspective. They may pull together a task force to investigate a significant safety issue or a noteworthy suggestion from a line technician. Their visit and subsequent actions endorse a No Compromise Safety Culture that blends company goals with operational capacities.

Leadership visits to job sites represent just one way to pay attention to hands-on operations. There are countless other ways to connect with workers in the field. One senior leader I know was just as effective in having one-on-ones with people away from the bustle of the worksite. Another preferred to host a monthly breakfast with small groups. Each created an opportunity for employees to express ideas or concerns and to ask questions. They shared the organization's path forward, and they encouraged honest feedback. They modeled desired leadership traits and, most importantly, they followed up as promised.

What gets measured gets done.

Once you establish routine communication with employees, you'll need to integrate the information you gather with safety metrics. In the transmission and distribution industry, one natural way to measure safety metrics is to break up the business into three categories of work: operations and maintenance, construction, and repair. Many organizations spread safety dollars and resources evenly between these buckets. If you begin to measure the safety performance of each area separately, you may find that you need to allocate resources differently.

For example, in maintenance work, which includes routine upgrades, we see higher recordable rates of injury because routine often leads to complacency. Construction safety is more challenging because the work consists of new builds. The high return on equity can cause managers and crews to speed up work to meet or exceed deadlines, leading to more mistakes. When responding to natural disasters and storms, the amount of repair work may increase. Due to high customer demand, storm crews may work longer hours and for more consecutive days; it is well-documented that fatigue can lead to higher incident rates. When you consider a wide array of variables and track the numbers, it will become clear which buckets need more attention.

Measuring safety outcomes helps senior leaders take site visits, employee breakfast meetings, and similar engagement events to the next level.

Tracking and measuring outcomes brings attention and focus to the things that are going well and areas needing improvement. As a result, senior leaders will shift their efforts to the bucket that is leaking. Managers and frontline leaders will focus on the bucket that represents their area. Managers will share this information with their direct reports, and everyone will begin to recognize their safety matters to company leadership.

As time goes on, crew managers adopt the methods successfully cultivated by and in successful teams. Crew leaders validate safe behaviors and reestablish or find ways to change weak ones. The further you look back at how safety has evolved, the more you can develop beyond your current challenges. The good news is that there is no additional expense in monitoring numbers you already have. A good spreadsheet can create trend lines and forecasting in safety performance and allow teams to identify potential problems sooner, making it easier to change negative trends.

Cultivate leaders continuously.

It is essential to identify the real leaders in your organization. Successful organizations grow and prosper financially and in safety performance by cultivating future leaders. An organization I know calls this program "Next Person Up." Each leader identifies and grooms another person in the company to take over their own job. Meanwhile, their manager or another leader grooms them for their next role. There are many great reasons why this is an effective business decision.

Organizations prefer to promote from within because their culture already exists in the individual. It creates smooth transitions, and the company's institutional knowledge stays intact. Promoting from within also creates an opportunity for upward mobility for all employees and skills redundancy between levels. Managers have a go-to person to help cover urgent needs when they are away. Employees see an opportunity for growth and promotion, which may lead to a more prosperous life. Everyone experiences the investment of ongoing training.

Most importantly, grooming future leaders promotes positive safety performance. When every person in an organization mentors another, a commitment to safety culture becomes multi-generational. There are more opportunities to talk about and teach others about safety with a single unified voice and message. Employees indirectly manage up and down the organization as they meet with both their mentor and their mentee.

Maintain a committed, visible focus on safety.

To maintain a committed, visible focus on safety, ask yourself, what is my organization doing (or not doing) to promote a culture of safety? Are we running a reactive or proactive safety culture? Is safety only mentioned when there's an incident? Do we begin meetings with a discussion of safety? How are we integrating safety into every part of the organization?

It's hard to visibly manage safety through email.

Most leaders in an organization will tell you their email inbox stays full. Managing email has become a daunting, ominous task. They wrangle it down every day, only to find it full a few hours later. It's frustrating for the leader and the people working with them. People expect an instant response. They see email as the magic wand of communication and behavior change. "I sent an email telling everyone to do it this way. Why didn't they do what I said?" Putting too much emphasis on email takes our focus off other company priorities, especially safety.

It's easy to give in to the trap of correspondence and communication. Many of us pride ourselves on finishing the day with an empty email box. We see managing our emails as managing our work. The question is are we managing our emails, or are our emails managing us? The task you choose to do becomes your priority, even if it's less critical. Is focusing on email (or some other low-priority goal) preventing you from paying attention to what's happening around you? What if an incident occurs in your area? When your manager asks, "What have you been doing to prevent this," do you really want to say, "Sending emails."?

Prioritize your work to meet safety goals.

Step back and think about your day, week, month, quarter, and year-end goals. Does answering emails (or doing some other administrative activity) immediately help you get there? Are you allowing the people who send you emails to control your time? What part of your routine is holding you back? How can you more efficiently meet your professional and safety goals? We know we can't stop answering emails, ignore text messages, or only tell people what we want in person; we should prioritize effective communication over fast, redundant communication.

The first step is to understand your audience and figure out the most effective way to communicate with them. Ask others, "How would you like for me to contact you? When do you want to hear about something?" If your manager prefers a single summary email at the end of the week, that's what you need to provide. Conversely, be sure to tell others the most effective way to communicate with you.

Pay attention to those who work for you. If your direct reports respond best to in-person meetings, consider more one-on-one interactions. Your job responsibilities and goals should drive how you allocate your time. Think, plan, execute, and follow-up your work to manage an influx of emails, text messages, phone calls, meetings, or any other kind of communication that bogs you down.

It's not what happens; it's how we react to what happens.

Some leaders spend their time and energy putting out fires instead of preventing them. They identify problems and react to them. They need to move equipment to another site; it's time to do random drug screening; they have an unexpected absence in staffing.

How can we expect employees to work strategically if they are too busy to see what is happening in the organization? We want everyone to pause and think instead of running around like their hair is on fire. We want people to react promptly when there's a significant problem. What would happen if we could prevent these problems altogether? Leaders could focus on business strategy, people development, efficiency, customer service, and *safety*. They would have time to anticipate common problems, including moving equipment, drug screening, and absences, *before* they happened. **They would have time to** progress toward safer operations. When we spend our days putting our fires, we can't move forward strategically. Those same fires will likely burn again tomorrow. If everyone takes an encompassing view of the organization, they can identify and change this circuitous behavior. Managers can recognize overwhelmed employees. Direct reports can see when they need to offer to help. Leaders can adjust their daily priorities to meet goals and prevent the fires that steal our attention.

Many years ago, I was at a business lunch with a colleague at a popular restaurant. This restaurant was bustling with people, including a sizable group. Everyone on the wait staff was hustling to deliver food, refill drinks, and clear tables. In between conversations about current safety issues, my colleague pointed out something intriguing.

He said, "Look at that server with those three tables." I saw this person running around with a water pitcher in one hand and dirty plates in another. They looked harried and frustrated. One of their tables had four people staring at dirty dishes. The second had two people trying to get the server's attention so they could order. At the third table sat a group of six people in need of drink refills. All this server could do was *react* to the circumstances.

Then my colleague said, "Now look at the server over there with the large group." The server for the large group was smiling and chatting with customers while refilling tea and water glasses, looking focused and calm. They appeared to anticipate requests before the customers asked. They glided around the tables with smooth, calculated movements.

"Wow," I said. "That server has twice as many people but looks completely in control." The second server even had time to pop over to the harried server's tables and refill drinks on their way back to the kitchen. Both servers had the same amount of work to do. What made the server for the large group look so calm and in control? That server thought proactively about the task at hand and the next necessary step. They planned efficiency into their work. They executed in a specific order to make sure they met customers' needs. By taking these forward-thinking actions, the calm server made their job more manageable and successful by doing it intentionally and professionally.

You cannot speak it into existence; you must manage it into reality.

Over the years, I've mentored numerous people in safety leadership roles who, after an incident, said, "Well, I told them not to do it that way." We know from frontline leader truths that you are responsible for your team's actions, even when you are away. How do you make sure your team understands what you want them to do? You manage it. You cannot teach a new skill or behavior solely by writing an email, telling them to do it a certain way, or creating a new policy. In fact, you may need to do all three of these things and more to teach someone a new behavior.

What is acceptable risk?

In transmission and distribution, construction, manufacturing, and other high-risk industries, we often set a goal of zero incidents. We never want to see an incident, especially a serious one. We also recognize that zero incidents is challenging goal to achieve and sustain because nothing we do is risk-free. Even a tiny splinter in your hand is considered an incident.

We should shoot for zero incidents in the same way a championship team wants to maintain a no-losing streak. We cannot mistakenly think we can achieve and sustain zero incidents forever; that simply is not realistic. We must understand there is an acceptable level of risk in everything we do. To prevent a fall injury in the company hallway, we could wrap everyone in bubble wrap, but that's not practical. We identify and mitigate as many risks as possible. We could post "slippery when wet" signs until the floor dries. We train the person cleaning the floors to leave a dry path for others to use. In this way, we have created an acceptable level of risk with the lowest risk environment possible. This environment leads us toward zero incidents in the most effective way.

The balance of safety.

In safety—much like our personal lives—there is a balance. We identify things in our lives that can affect our safety performance. Many things can shift the balance of safety: the start of summer vacation, the weather, or a problem at home. When we take our focus away from the task at hand, we increase the amount of risk. We are more likely to rush or make decisions and errors that lead to an incident. At both the office and in the field, leaders in the organization should anticipate events that could cause imbalanced thinking and plan ways to counterbalance them. We must adapt for balance in the same way we adapt operations, personnel, equipment, and other variables to each job.

Continue communication.

As previously noted, communication is critical. Communicate the imbalance in a proactive, positive way. "We know you're excited about the holidays. Please stay focused on your work so you can get home safely to enjoy this time with your loved ones." You can communicate anticipated events through newsletters, weekly briefings, social media, and internal communications. Carve out additional time in meetings, job briefings, and ongoing training to mention the balance of safety. You may put an extra eye on the employee who is doing hot work or a critical task. You may stop unsafe work and talk about what was unsafe. You may remind everyone to be each other's keeper during this time.

Maintain ownership through involvement.

Promoting a balance of safety can be the perfect opportunity for managers and senior leaders to step into the field to show support for crews. Make sure your high expectations are not unintentionally suggesting teams make bad decisions to meet your goals. You must make the effort to ensure your audience understands what you are trying to convey. One way to communicate effectively is *not* making assumptions about others' knowledge, skills, and abilities. You cannot assume everyone knows about and is preparing for the imbalance you see. Some researchers call this behavior the curse of knowledge. People with a wealth of accumulated knowledge sometimes think everyone else knows the same things they know. They either communicate in all-encompassing, vague phrases, or they fail to communicate at all.

Creating the lowest risk environment possible requires considerable focus, tools, processes, and commitment at all levels. You can accomplish a low-risk environment by maintaining ownership of your area and communicating both up and down the chain of command.

This is especially important for frontline leaders. Pay attention to what's happening. Ensure that safety is always a part of your planning and metrics. Be accountable for your area and the work of employees who report to you. If you need to lower risk more, communicate your need for help to your manager. Understand there are many subcultures in every organization and no two crews are the same. Different divisions and regions may have a unique culture that coincides with their way of working; a crew in the deep south faces challenges distinct from those who work in the snowy north. Use these differences as opportunities to understand alternative ways of doing things.

Summary of Safety Truth #6: Pay attention to what's going on in your organization.

Paying attention to what is happening in your organization is part of our path to achieve a No Compromise Safety Culture. It's a comprehensive approach to connect strategic business goals with important safety goals. It is an opportunity to involve everyone from the top of the organization to the individual contributor. Highlight positive events to connect with employees on a personal level and anticipate and prevent problems that have the potential to impact a No Compromise culture. Show your colleagues you value safety because you value them. Recognize that where you place your time and energy is where you'll get results.

Everyone must own safety for No Compromise Safety Culture to work.

A No Compromise Safety Culture is a shared vision. It relies on an integrated approach that includes ownership, responsibility, and accountability by all employees.

When senior leaders contact me for help in changing their safety culture, I always ask, "How serious are you about this?" I'm not talking about how much money they're willing to spend on safety, although that is often their first thought.

It's not that at all. I ask instead, "Are you willing to do the work to change the established culture? Are you willing to own safety at every level? Do you have the courage to listen to what your employees are saying about you?" I want to know if they are committed enough to make this shift by devoting their time, adjusting their priorities, and changing their thought processes to create a No Compromise Safety Culture.

Next, I ask for their safety numbers to study how they are performing relative to their industry. How are they trending? Are the issues systemic or found in individual crews? How does the company use those numbers to improve its safety performance?

Third, I ask employees to complete a survey to understand their perspective on the organization's culture. What do the employees think about the organization's approach to safety? Does the company share safety-related data with employees? Is there a perception that the company values dollars over safety? Is safety apparent in the day-to-day messaging coming from the organization? In companies with above-average recordable injury rates, I ask, "Are you expected to focus on safety? Does top leadership understand the safety numbers? Do employees see safety as a barrier to work or as a part of the work? Is safety a token phrase, or is it a real value in the organization?"

Ownership

For a No Compromise Safety Culture to work, all employees must own a piece of the safety pie. Those in the field steer safety performance by recognizing and controlling hazards. Upper management wants field leadership to take ownership of safety by managing equipment, projects, and people. Similarly, employees in corporate roles drive safety by incorporating safety-based decisions and actions on a daily basis. To facilitate ownership across organizations, we must empower both leaders and employees. Employees need expectations, and leaders need to listen to employees. Each individual should have intentional thoughts and actions about safety so that they naturally own and address issues before they turn into incidents and injuries.

Implement an integrated approach.

The best way to achieve ownership is to use an integrated approach in which every person considers safety in every business segment. Planning and making decisions based on a safety mindset creates opportunities to build in processes that change outcomes. In organizations where safety weaves throughout the company, creating and sustaining a safe work environment is a cultural expectation. Everyone recognizes the benefits of having an integrated safety culture that isn't limited to a stand-alone safety department or a prepackaged program.

For example, when corporate communications integrate with safety, they weave the safety message into all communications. The culture is about doing all things safely because "that's how we do it here." As a No Compromise culture evolves, the safety department becomes less of an independent group and more entwined throughout the organization.

The key to creating an integrated approach is *not* compromising safety, it's broadening the scope and expectation throughout the company. Safety becomes a guidepost when facing challenges related to budget constraints, deadlines, peer pressure, complacency, and customer demands. In a No Compromise culture, we incorporate safety into all aspects of work, whether planning, bidding, hiring contractors, or executing the job. Safety must be everyone's priority to achieve maximum results.

Manage expectations.

It is easy to view safety in a negative, critical, and reactive way. At the beginning of a No Compromise safety journey, you cannot expect to go from a ten recordable rate to one overnight. It would be best to manage the expectation that progress will take collaboration, process improvement, development, and time. Be realistic about where you are in the process journey. Examine your culture and identify where you are now and where you want to be. Safety is complex and nuanced, making it difficult to measure. You will need to decide the best metrics for your industry and how you will track them. Start with the safety rate of the industry in general. How do you compare? Do you want to be top quartile or even top decile? Do you need to lower your recordable rate to meet the standards of a potential customer?

Focus on the things you can do immediately and use your previous safety performance to set manageable goals. Keep your goals and metrics simple so everyone understands the focus and plan to achieve the goals. Communicate small wins early and often so everyone can see the benefits of a No Compromise Safety Culture.

Pay attention to the right things. How are employees getting hurt? Examine the processes that make up the operational history of the company. Which tasks have the most incidents? What needs immediate attention? After you set a goal and determine how to measure it, share this plan throughout the organization. Make sure everyone is accountable for this goal. Set the expectation that everyone should focus on improving the culture of safety. Manage this expectation with clearly communicated, thoughtful, attainable goals.

The power of the positive strikes yet again!

When your organization rolls out a No Compromise Safety Culture, expect people to challenge it immediately. Everything you do, from choosing specific safety goals to rolling out the plan, needs to be communicated and implemented in an open, positive, and holistic way. Instead of finding fault, look for ways to prevent the recurrence of past incidents. You *can* create a positive safety environment by accentuating what is going well. Focus on catching people doing things right. How can a department help meet this safety goal? How can we prevent this incident next time? What is holding us back? It's tempting to look at incidents as a failure in safety, but it doesn't have to be that way. An optimistic view is particularly enlightening when you examine the details of an incident.

You have a choice: You can respond to an incident in a disapproving, morale-busting way; you can start throwing out blame; or you can ignore small things and wait for them to develop into big things. But a more effective way to deal with an incident is to look at it as a learning opportunity—acknowledge the incident, figure out the root cause, and create a solution to prevent it next time.

We always strive for zero incidents. In reality, things happen. No winning streak lasts forever. The key to moving forward is to handle adverse events in the most positive way. Remember, creating a No Compromise Safety Culture is not a destination. It's a journey.

Safety is a personal mindset.

Expert ability without passion is not as effective as amateur ability with passion. Early in my football and wrestling coaching careers, I discovered that the greatest players on the team were not defined simply by their ability. They stood out because of their attitude, motivation, and determination to win. They enjoyed the sport and had fun with it. They developed the emotional intelligence to appreciate where they were in their journey. They worked harder to meet personal goals because they understood the benefits of focused effort.

The same applies to building a culture of No Compromise. Everyone in the organization needs to be committed and working toward the safety goal. We want the procurement team to understand safety as it relates to people in the call center, meter readers, and the line technicians. Developing this mindset can take time. Sometimes our work is so specialized we don't see the connection between our department and other areas of the organization. We don't always think about how our work affects safety. Help teams connect the dots between safety, their department, and other departments. Be creative. Start all meetings with a discussion of safety and recognize top-notch safety performances. Communicate and enforce safety expectations to everyone. Include safety in all business plans and job bids and add safety performance to all employee job descriptions and customer evaluations.

Unintended positive impacts.

The beauty of a No Compromise Safety Culture is the unintended positive effects it creates. When everyone integrates safety into their division of the business, the resulting lower-risk environment translates into fewer incidents. Fewer incidents interrupting our work makes us more efficient and customer-focused. Valuing safety becomes a synergistic, self-fulfilling prophecy.

As employees begin to see and feel the benefits of working in a low-risk environment, they grow the No Compromise Safety Culture through everyday decisions and actions. Employees develop an attitude of enthusiasm for safety. They willingly embrace known safety procedures and policies that reflect operational discipline and fundamental safety practices. They notice the little wins, and this increases morale and participation. Teamwork and collaboration increase as people who are not directly involved in this safety movement decide to participate. Momentum builds as the safety numbers improve. We see greater employee engagement, satisfaction, and pride. When I witnessed a customer service department asking for information as they made plans for safety, I knew we had integrated safety throughout the organization. If your culture matures so far that people start reminding each other about safety, you have begun to operate a No Compromise Safety Culture.

Change affects safety.

In safety, your job never stops. The only constant in life is change. There will always be employee turnover, contract changes, new procedures, additional risks, and technical advancements.

But change can be difficult for some people. We all prefer routines, and we create them for almost everything we do. We need to understand how change is going to affect safety in our operations. We prepare for this eventuality and adjust our safety plans, routines, and communications accordingly. Employees need to be ready for changes. Events such as short-staffing or storm work may create the need to combine two different crews into one. This change of plans interrupts routines as everyone becomes comfortable with their new role. During this time, it's imperative we have clear, precise communication about assigned roles and not lose focus on safety.

Even small changes in the internal organization, the workforce, or the work environment can threaten safety. People get preoccupied with activities going on in their lives, which can lead to distractions and injuries. The most exemplary performance can turn upside down in a split second. This downturn may be due to a failure to follow procedures or an inability to recognize hazards, distractions, attitude, complacency, and false security based on past success. We must realize the same process that worked yesterday does not work under today's conditions. Part of owning your work includes adjusting strategies and modifying behavior proactively. To persuade others to make this change, reinforce it as a professional adaptation. We can use change to highlight good behaviors and create even stronger ones. Understanding that change affects safety—no matter how small or large—requires us to stay focused on the task, much like defensive driving requires us to scan the road ahead and check our mirrors continuously.

Anticipate and prepare for change.

Leadership must focus on safety as a core business value and an operational priority while keeping safety at the forefront through awareness and education. The more you know about the workings of an organization, the better you will be at meeting the organization's needs.

Unexpected changes in the economy or the weather can create an entirely new business and operational situation. You may experience changes in your area of responsibility, such as moving to a variable workforce, changing physical locations, or hiring a sudden surge of contractors. You may work with a various cultures within and outside your organization or be planning a significant business move like a merger or an acquisition. In all these scenarios, safety should remain an up-front priority. Everyone in the organization should see the focus on safety as the priority that never changes.

Change highlights weak processes.

During periods of change, weak safety processes rear their ugly heads. Bad habits we got away with for years without incident now cause problems. It's easy to overlook that emotionally-charged changes, such as rightsizing, affect safety. Let's say your company restructures and offers early retirement to several long-term employees. These employees know the company and their roles inside out. After this change is complete, you realize that the person who was the National Electrical Safety Code expert at your company is gone. It will take you hours of research to find an answer this person could have provided in minutes. The weakness of not having a secondary expert or an effective succession plan creates a challenge to comply with this code.

Identify and control inefficient processes.

One of the best ways to identify and control inefficient processes is to look out for change and potential change. Change is the number one factor increasing risk in an organization. The method you used in the past to achieve a specific result may not work in times of change because some element is now different.

Even the simplest, most familiar changes can affect safety. Is your crew changing locations, equipment, or tasks? Even if you've completed a particular task without incident for the last twenty years, not managing a change in the system or routine can increase the risk. Change often takes away our safety net. When a friend on a job changes crews, they are no longer there to cover for you. The small things your teammate used to do are now fall on you; when was the last time you did them? We must always plan for something to go wrong. What is our primary defense? What is our secondary defense? As you study your safety record and processes, you can identify procedures weakened by an anticipated change. Be proactive. Figure out how to identify and strengthen weak processes.

We cannot assume safety will take care of itself.

In too many industries, we often promote technically proficient people and then mistakenly think safety and leadership will take care of themselves. We believe once safety is mastered, it doesn't require the same effort to maintain that mastery.

In fact, when leadership roles change, it often takes *more* time because change can become a barrier. In the shuffle of reorganizing, we can inadvertently take our focus off the culture of safety. Reconfigured teams need to establish a new rhythm. New team leaders need to talk about safety first because it reiterates that safety is a constant that drives all the other things we want to accomplish. They must engage the entire team with discussions about what could happen and seek answers to resolve potential problems.

During my safety journey, I advanced from a safety professional into an operations manager role. My promotion was a change that caused me to give safety less attention because there was always something else to manage. I was overwhelmed with new skills, tasks, and responsibilities, and I assumed our high standards would take care of themselves. I quickly learned that safety doesn't work that way. We cannot check safety off the list, move on to the next task, and expect safety to remain a value. The thing that gets our attention gets results. When you take your attention off safety, even for a short time, it erodes the culture you have worked so hard to create.

Combining two companies into one culture.

The biggest challenge I experienced in getting employees to take ownership of safety was when my organization merged with another company. Combining two companies introduced a massive amount of change that created a significant risk factor to safety.

The first thing we did was pull together a task team to combine the operations policies and procedures of the two companies. People in both organizations recognized safety needed to continue to be a value. We wanted to find synergies, duplications, best practices, and small and large ways to improve operations. Our goal was to create "one utility."

At the onset, this reorganization seemed simple enough. We were now one company, committed to safety and speaking with one unified voice. Although we didn't want to generate additional risk by making unnecessary changes, we knew we would operate at peak performance once we established the best procedures from each organization into one. In reality, we had many other variables to consider. Both organizations had good safety records., but we accomplished these records using different safety policies and procedures. Established patterns and habits were hard to blend into a single method. As we began to make changes, we saw resentment from both sides, who saw their way as the best way. People wondered, "Why change something that's working?"

Along with the challenge of creating one utility, we needed to combine two different safety manuals into one, which introduced a lot of change and upheaval in the organization. As safety professionals, we needed to figure out how to manage that change and maintain a sense of ownership during this process. We needed to decide what safety rules we would use and how we would ensure compliance. After much work, we settled on a final draft and released the new manual to the new organization.

Although we were authorized to combine the two manuals, the rollout and execution of the new safety manual was not as strong as it should have been. After receiving the new safety manual with different processes, workers continued to do things as they had in the previous, stand-alone company. Employees from each utility thought their manual was gospel. Each side assumed the way they had done things for twenty years was still the best way. Our operations and safety task team soon realized you could not write something in a manual and expect change. You cannot speak it into existence. Without a solid implementation process, even the best plans will not get done.

Fortunately, we were able to regroup. We sent safety people into the field to meet with operational leaders to understand the impacts of the manual changes. We asked questions and involved more people so we could identify and fix procedural weaknesses. We stepped up our coaching and training efforts and asked frontline leaders to help us drive the implementation of the new manual. We involved corporate communications to make sure we promoted the new manual through multiple channels. In the end, our integrated effort paid off as we fostered collaboration and ownership in the new organization.

Manage change.

Another significant change I experienced was when my company bought a smaller organization with a lower safety record. We intuitively thought the other company's record would rise to the same level as ours, and ours would remain the same. We thought everyone would gravitate to our higher standard.

Neither of those things happened. Just like establishing a No Compromise Safety Culture, combining two different company cultures takes time. It's like mixing hot and cold water and expecting something other than warm. Again, we had to manage the cultural shift. We began with buy-in from leadership in both organizations. Then we communicated with teams and crews and adopted best practices from both organizations. We knew we could not immediately push our new partners into changing behavior; we had to develop trust. We needed to listen. We wanted to frame things in a positive light. We had to approach this change with humility and servant leadership.

For major changes like mergers and acquisitions, draw from all the company resources you can. Gather safety, change management, and communications professionals, and ask them to help plan and communicate the change through positive messages to employees. Identify gaps and figure out ways to close them. Pull in the right people and resources you need to think, plan, execute, and expect changes as the plan evolves.

Summary of Safety Truth #7: Everyone must own safety for a No Compromise Safety Culture to work.

Safety isn't just the job of the safety department or even the employees who work in the highest risk environment. Safety is *everyone's* job. We must approach it with an integrated approach that encourages ownership at every level. Everyone should think of safety as inherent in the way they do business. When we talk about safety, we need to speak with one voice. Everyone needs to understand how, why, and when to do it. We want everyone to see how safety benefits them and how a No Compromise Safety Culture increases morale and profitability. When we have complete ownership of safety in an organization, it becomes an overlay of the entire company. Even when there's change, effective safety remains the same.

Each and every person in the company has an important safety role.

_____

Everyone in the organization must understand how their role contributes to world-class safety performance. To identify and resolve gaps in performance, look to the next level of leadership until you find the weak link.

Lead like a goose—or go to the back and honk like one.

You've probably seen a group of geese flying in a V-formation. It's fascinating to realize they fly in this formation for safety and efficiency. It's safer because they can see and keep track of each other and communicate through honking. It's efficient because the V-formation reduces wind resistance and helps conserve energy. Humans mimic this instinctive formation in cycling and flying fighter planes. Even more interesting is that, when flying in a skein, the geese support one another and the lead goose through their loud honking. When the lead goose gets tired, another takes over.

What can we learn from geese flying in formation? Like the lead goose, somebody must take the lead in safety to break the wind and make things safer for the other people on the team. To be most efficient, everyone on the team must support the person in the lead. In safety, a leader is most effective when supported by others and less so without the support of the whole team. If you're not in a lead role, jump into formation and honk like heck for the lead goose, and you will eventually get your turn in the lead of the formation.

Safety roles

We know from Safety Truth #7 that everyone in the organization must own safety for No Compromise Safety Culture to work, but how do we determine each person's *role* in safety? In precision military operations, everyone precisely knows their role and what to expect from everyone else. They operate using a specific model based on thinking, planning, execution, and follow-up. Each member of the team is prepared to assume the duties of their supervisor. Their very lives hinge on each person operating as efficiently and safely as possible. This clearly defined structure pays off, particularly in combat and high-risk operations. In safety, it is equally important that everyone understands their role and how they will execute it. They need to know what their teammates are doing and how they will work in tandem. They need to understand their manager's role and how to support the manager.

Management's safety role in achieving a No Compromise Safety Culture

Organizations that operate with specific safety protocols usually have clearly defined roles in their safety manuals and job descriptions, beginning with a conspicuous definition of the organization's safety goals. For example, they may say, "The company's goal is to complete each job and workday without personal injury, vehicle incident, or damage to company or other property." From there, safety-focused organizations define the expectations of leadership team members, supervisors, and individual contributors. They explicitly state how they expect each employee to set a personal commitment by adhering to all applicable safety rules. By identifying, cultivating, and promoting safety-minded employees into leadership positions, management demonstrates its commitment to those who embrace their safety goals. Organizational leaders are responsible for providing employees opportunities to acquire the technical and leadership skills needed to work efficiently and safely. Managers also supply well-maintained equipment and tools that permit employees to complete their assigned tasks without creating or exposing themselves or others to unnecessary hazards.

The safety director's safety role

Regardless of where they fall in a company's organizational chart, the safety director ensures the workforce has the knowledge and skills to work safely. Safety directors provide management with guidance in safety-related areas required by state or federal law and craft company policies that are functional and achievable. They assist production management and supervision with identifying and resolving safety hazards presented by either projected work or work in progress and serve as the company's primary contact for compliance and incident investigations. Safety professionals visit work areas regularly to observe work practices and equipment and to promote safe work attitudes. They provide training and coaching to ensure everyone has the knowledge and skills necessary to perform their work in the safest way possible.

The frontline leader's safety role

The next position in safety responsibility is the frontline leader, including crew leaders or anyone in charge of a job site. These leaders set a personal example by following all applicable safety rules. They train and coach the men and women on their crew to be certain they have the job skills needed to work safely and efficiently. Frontline leaders work in tandem with field safety directors to meet the company's safety goals by identifying and eliminating unsafe work practices and ensuring all potential travel and field safety hazards are eliminated or effectively managed. They enforce the company's safety and disciplinary policies to create respect for people and documented standards.

As technology, capabilities, staff, and expectations evolve, you will need to assess and update roles in safety manuals and job descriptions. Keep in mind the substantial legal ramifications of these documents. Some people believe that holding employees accountable for safety in writing through job descriptions and safety manuals creates a greater liability, presuming, "What if we have a serious incident or fatality, and the plaintiff's attorneys subpoena these documents?" They rationalize that they are removing responsibility for safety by keeping safety roles out of these documents.

The opposite is true. If your organization has a serious incident or fatality, you are responsible for creating a safe workplace, even if you never mentioned it. In fact, not citing safety appears to as a flagrant disregard for safety and is considered a deceptive practice. Of all the things your organization is responsible for—profit margins, environmental concerns, regulatory changes—employee safety should always be at the top of the priority list. Each employee's role in safety must be definitively communicated, documented, and understood so everyone can take responsibility for their part.

Put the right people in the right positions.

Hire and promote people carefully. Just because a person performed successfully in a technical role for years doesn't mean that person is ready to take on a supervisory role. A line technician with a deep knowledge base of safety may not flourish at the frontline leader level. Understand that, even if you like a person who does not demonstrate proficiency in safety, you may still have to place that person in a different position for them to flourish. If this person flounders as a leader, everybody suffers, and a consequential negative outcome is quite real. In fact, people who promote too fast are often relieved to step back when they realize the weight and must have a proven, demonstrated proficiency for safety for each new position. Promote and hire people with the aptitude to perform all the knowledge, skills, and abilities outlined in the job description.

Provide clear guidance and expectations for each new advancement.

When you hire or promote someone, you have an obligation to that person and the company to help them perform effectively and safely. A newly promoted leader or supervisor should already have had the opportunity to lead and supervise under the watchful eye of a mentor. The easiest and most productive way to set employees up for success is to provide clear guidance, expectations, and mentored experience for their new role. Just because you change a person's title doesn't mean they automatically know how to do every aspect of the new job. You will need to continuously develop and coach that person to meet the expectations of the role. If someone is not performing effectively in a position, figure out why and fix it. Are you offering enough encouragement, training, and resources for that person to flourish?

Heads up, look inside and out, and keep blocking.

When I first started coaching football, our quarterback kept getting sacked. We needed to improve the offensive line's performance. I adopted a brilliant, complex blocking scheme and proudly introduced it at the next practice. Everyone on the offensive line said they understood it. When we tried to execute my dazzling new plan, the results were worse than before! Nobody seemed to know what to do. Each of the five blockers interpreted the role differently. After the ball snapped, the blockers hesitated; they weren't sure of what to do next. They lacked the confidence to implement the complex blocking scheme and failed to execute it.

We struggled to move the ball forward. We needed a plan with fewer contingencies—a plan that always stayed the same. I scrapped the complex scheme and went back to basics with a simple heads-up, inside, outside philosophy everyone understood immediately. I told them, "After the ball snaps, look straight in front of you and block that person. If nobody's in front of you, look to the inside and block that person. If nobody's on the inside, look to the outside and block that person." Our offensive line instantly started firing off the snap of the ball, which created our advantage. Everyone felt confident. They were able to execute. As a coach, it was my responsibility to lead the team with clear directives for each role. My job was to think, plan, implement, and follow-up. I learned a simple lesson that I still use today: When we overcomplicate a role, we lose focus on the desired result.

Cultivate leaders in safety.

At the beginning of this book, I shared how I started my career as a prison guard. After that, I became a schoolteacher and a coach. From there, I learned to be a telephone installer/repair technician. I was thirty-three years old when I finally found my true calling. I became a crew member on a utility crew and experienced the camaraderie and pride of working with a team of highly skilled professionals in a high-risk environment. Our team performed high-caliber work under extreme conditions to serve other people. We considered ourselves heroes who got the lights back on, kept the hospital running, and went into every storm to start the recovery from devastation.

I recognized and appreciated the coaching mentality of the leaders in the organization, especially the people who mentored me. When I was an early apprentice on a construction maintenance crew, my frontline supervisor taught me the guiding principles of safety each step along the way. For example, he taught me a simple way to stay focused while working with energized lines. He'd say, "Sheridan, what color is the dielectric cover hose?" I answered it was orange. Then he would say, "When you see orange, use that as a reminder that the line is energized." This fundamental yet straightforward safety concept helped me stay focused every time I worked with energized lines. He was able to engage me in learning, and his mentorship groomed me for my future career in safety.

It's essential to groom employees by continually training them to perform safely and prepare them for the next role. It's also important to groom yourself, not only to learn but to set an example for others. We perform at a higher standard when we know someone is learning from us. Our process should be: Learn it. Practice it. Teach it. When you cultivate others, you not only enhance the value of your organization, you showcase the additional value each person brings to the job site.

For example, a director can cultivate a frontline leader by asking them to help prepare a presentation for leadership. A frontline leader can coach crew members by teaching them how to lead a job briefing. A crew member can coach a new hire on safety. When everyone is learning and growing, the team becomes more cohesive. In a No Compromise Safety Culture, every leader's goal should be to have everyone on the team engaged in cultivating someone else.

Provide ongoing training.

Training is a crucial part of managing safety in organizations with high-risk environments and the potential for severe injuries and fatalities. Technology and procedures change continually, resulting in constant revisions of regulations and policies.

There are many ways to train employees to recognize hazards, develop skills to reduce risk, and remain mentally nimble to grow and adapt. The most effective way to achieve lasting results is to train people where they are in their journey. Personalize training for their particular role through formal and informal mentoring programs, individual coaching sessions with a supervisor, and time in the field. One safety professional I know weaves safety messages into internal communications that cascade throughout the company. They forecast changes in the environment that may be a threat to safety. One of their weekly video shorts in the fall/winter begins with, "We average ten deer strikes during deer hunting season." After identifying this weak data point, they offer simple, preventive measures. They suggest scanning the road ahead, watching more closely for deer at dawn and dusk, and anticipating more deer when you see only one. This safety message serves as a real-time teachable moment.

Identify performance gaps.

In organizations that lead with safety, managers understand a significant part of their role is to identify and fix performance gaps. It's self-sustaining to equip employees to succeed. If you don't support and lead in safety, you probably won't get the results you want. A weak link in the chain can affect peoples' lives in a significantly negative way. A decision you make or an action you take today may cause an incident months or years later.

When using a top-led, employee-driven safety model, you need to gather more data and review each role if you find you're not getting the results you expect. There may be a gap in effectiveness because someone is not performing their defined role as prescribed. A common problem in safety is when managers assume they can delegate a portion of their safety responsibilities. They hand over the safe operations of their crew to the safety department, but safety is responsible for supporting safe operations, not running safe operations.

This doesn't mean there cannot be a strong collaboration between managers and safety; it means managers must stay in charge of running daily operations. Safety should be a *resource* for managers and supervisors, not a replacement for them. In one organization I'm familiar with, a non-technical person advanced into a safety role. When they visited a job site, a crew leader asked them specific technical questions. This overzealous safety professional began trying to answer these operational questions. One thing led to another, and the visit evolved from a collaboration between safety and operations into an operational takeover by safety. The safety professional inadvertently began to do the crew leader's job, blurring the line between each role's responsibilities and weakening both positions. Although this example sounds minor, the ripple effect can be substantial. How can a safety professional continue to manage their responsibilities throughout the organization if they've just assumed the duties of a crew leader? How can the crew leader *lead* the team if they've given away their responsibility for employee safety?

Safety performance gaps frequently begin at the leadership level.

When organizations hire me to help develop a No Compromise Safety Culture, I often begin with a gap analysis. I identify the weak link in safety and analyze each role to pinpoint the performance gap. I start at the problem and work my way up the leadership chain to identify the weak performance link. That point is where I begin to solve the problem.

As we compare performance among similar groups, we begin to see patterns. Safety performance issues typically occur when an employee does not fully execute the responsibility of their role. Often the problem is a reflection or result of poor management from above. What is the root cause of poor safety performance? What has the poor performer's manager done—or not done—to get the expected results? Is this manager bogged down with responsibilities that take away from a focus on safety? Does the poor performer understand their role in safety? To create and sustain a No Compromise Safety Culture, leaders must value safety, and their behaviors must focus on positive safety performance in every role.

We tend to focus our skills on our areas of strength. Many company leaders excel in analyzing numbers and building spreadsheets, but they may not be proficient in safety and technical integration. They may avoid field visits because they feel insecure about not being a technical expert. My message to them: Don't let your ego get in the way of expanding your knowledge base. You can make the most significant gains in your organization by learning from the employees in the field. This personal development allows you to create checks and balances in the organization. It enables employees to highlight their professional knowledge and skills.

One SVP colleague of mine visited job sites regularly and wanted to make sure they didn't violate any safety protocols during the visit. They asked for a crew member to escort them for safety and share proper safety procedures and practices. The employees were proud to teach the boss's boss about safety. This SVP listened carefully and took notes. After the visit, they always called me to ask questions and talk strategy. They made sure they understood what was happening on the site that day. They didn't want to miss any small details or major corrections. The SVP understood the value of building a solid safety culture in the field, and their actions reflected this value.

The shadow you cast falls on others.

The way you live your life and do your work—even if you're not in a leadership role—influences the behavior of at least seven people. Those seven people influence seven more people, who influence another seven people, and so on. It is possible you impact the course of behavior well beyond your immediate circle. That's a big responsibility, particularly when it comes to safety. Think about the people in your organization you influence—the people who see you as a leader in safety. If you had a video of one of those people on the job behaving the way you taught them, wouldn't you feel proud to see your hard work in action? One SVP told me, "As a leader, I'm busy. I'm hit with requests from employees from all over the country on a daily basis. I need to meet those employee requests. At the same time, I have to make sure I do not compromise safety by losing my visible commitment to safety." This leader understood the value of being a visible, positive, influential leader.

Your actions speak louder than your words.

It's crucial for people in influential positions to lead with actions as well as words. People watch and learn from you whether you intend to teach them or not. Occasionally, I'll come across a situation where a person in a leadership position makes a poor judgment call on safety behavior. For example, a crew was working on a primary conductor caught under branches in a residential neighborhood. There was a digger truck with the extended boom in the vicinity. In an effort to apply a quick fix, a superintendent walked out on the boom without fall protection and grabbed a non-grounded wire while wearing leather work gloves instead of the required rubber gloves.

Fortunately, this careless act did not result in an incident. It did, however, place the entire safety culture in jeopardy. Although the superintendent regretted this behavior, there was no taking it back. An apprentice happened to catch the entire scene on video with a mobile phone. With at least fifteen people watching, how many more cell phones do you think recorded it? This leader lost all credibility up and down the organization's chain of command.

How can this supervisor expect to be a safety leader after this blatant disregard for safety protocols? It's disrespectful and dishonest to the people you lead and the organization as a whole. Among the many safety lessons we learned from this event, the most important was that actions speak louder than words. When events like this occurred in an organization I supported, I stepped back to identify my personal accountability that may have enabled a leader to make such a lapse in judgment. What were the failures in our safety process that allowed this behavior? Why didn't we recognize this poor performer sooner? Is this rogue safety performance a personnel issue, or is it systemic?

Summary of Safety Truth #8: Every person in the company has a safety role.

To achieve a world-class safety performance, everyone on the team must perform in concert. Like a well-organized offensive line, an influential safety culture must have well-defined, clearly articulated roles for each team member. Provide clear expectations for achieving the safety results you expect in all job descriptions and the safety manual. Make sure everyone understands and owns their roles. Understand the impact leaders in the organization have on safety. Develop all employees into leaders with ongoing coaching and training. If your organization has a poor safety performance, look at yourself first. Results are a reflection of leadership; what part of your leadership is not fulfilling the expectations of your role? After identifying the root cause of the gap, think, plan, execute, and follow-up with a solution.

Safety is not just about you.

―――――――

When a No Compromise Safety Culture permeates every area of an organization, stakeholders begin to view safety beyond the scope of their everyday activities. Companies experience the synergistic effect of collaboration and momentum.

Safety is about the people who influence it.

The most gratifying part of creating a No Compromise Safety Culture is when we begin to see people throughout the organization leading with safety. Professionals from accounting ask themselves, "How can we meet this financial goal while keeping safety a priority?" New employees feel comfortable asking safety questions during job briefings. Senior leaders ask frontline leaders, "What can we do to help you meet safety goals?" Safety is a permanent line item in budgets, an agenda item in meetings, and a goal in training. Everyone considers safety *first*. They seamlessly integrate safety goals into their job responsibilities and projects. They behave as safety *influencers*.

An effective way to cultivate safety influencers at all levels is through internal and external communications. Effective communication makes safety visible and tangible. It drives safety messages to multiple audiences. Safety professionals partner with corporate communications to brand safety in internal communications with specific campaigns utilizing intranet and newsletter articles, internal signage, senior leader messaging, and company events. The external communications team distributes messaging through social media, branding campaigns, external presentations, and press releases. Your communications partners incorporate safety as an objective in communications plans, editorial calendars, budgets, company events, and year-end metrics.

Safety influencers often come from the most unpredictable places. For example, someone in payroll who grew up next door to an injured line technician could turn out to be one of your best safety influencers. I worked closely with a communications professional who became such a safety advocate that she routinely asked our safety department to review written communications and photos before publication. You can cultivate these influencer relationships by asking these professionals to help develop a No Compromise culture. Look for people with high emotional intelligence who are willing to admit their mistakes, learn from others, and move forward after an incident. Colleagues with high emotional intelligence can read the room; they listen intently, empathize with others, and choose their words carefully. They see themselves as servant leaders and strive to lift the people around them. They share successes and accept responsibility for failures. They recognize the many benefits of a No Compromise Safety Culture and work purposefully to achieve it.

At the beginning of my safety journey, my managers began cultivating me as a safety influencer. They recognized my experience in teaching and created opportunities for me to present at safety meetings. I advanced from crew member to journeyman lineman to service manager, safety consultant, and an operational district manager. I drew from my education in health, sociology, and psychology, nurtured it with continuing education in safety, and successfully taught coaching methods to educate and persuade others.

As I learned more about safety, the industry, and operations, I began to see the need for a company-wide, integrated approach. Just like a well-crafted business plan, an integrated safety approach starts with the end in mind. Senior leaders began to value the need to protect people and property, reduce liability, and comply with and exceed OSHA standards and federal laws. To accomplish these goals, we engaged every corporate resource by integrating all organizational departments and all employees. We successfully navigated a cultural shift; we created an integrated No Compromise Safety Culture.

Develop a No Compromise Safety Culture in three stages.

To shape the No Compromise methodology for organizational safety development, I used psychology theories, behavioral strategies, and personal experience, all of which have been presented in the previous eight safety truths. It took time and dedicated work from many people to implement. To begin, we needed to understand how people viewed and responded to unsafe conditions. We knew our instincts helped us avoid getting hurt—we naturally flee danger. We use our senses to smell smoke, feel heat, hear sirens, and recognize the imminent threat of fire. In most industries, however, instincts are not enough to keep us safe. We must learn, understand, and integrate behaviors to create and sustain a No Compromise Safety Culture. Safety becomes an uncompromising core principle in our value system achievable through three significant stages of development.

STAGE 1: LEARN

In Stage 1 of developing a No Compromise Safety Culture, safety transitions from a fleeting thought in a task-based function into a core value. We create the organization's guiding documents—the policies, procedures, and safety manuals. We learn to depend on others to help keep us safe, and we reciprocate in kind. We begin to recognize what we should and should not do. We relearn boundaries and rules, and we comply because our managers have fully demonstrated a commitment to and an expectation for a No Compromise Safety Culture. We begin by thinking about safety in terms of ourselves but soon evolve to understand a safe working environment is not an individual concern. It's similar to how a visitor to a job site may know to wear a hard hat but needs guidance to stay clear of the line of fire.

At this tactical stage, we rely heavily on others to teach and supervise us, and managers rely heavily on procedures and enforcement. To be successful, we must be willing to listen and to learn. Leaders must think, plan, execute, and follow-up with us. As an organization, we use this stage to gather and interpret safety data and set safety goals and metrics for multiple divisions. We make sure everyone understands their new roles and responsibilities for creating the lowest risk environment. We communicate safety in a way that makes it easy to understand and implement.

STAGE 2: UNDERSTAND

In Stage 1, we learn the benefits of safety and the procedures for achieving the lowest risk environment. As we move into Stage 2, we begin to see the big picture. In this phase of personal awareness, we become independent. We have attained genuine insight about following the rules because we understand *why*. We no longer need anyone to convince us to wear hearing protection; we have experienced firsthand the benefits of wearing it. We see, feel, and understand the positive outcomes of safety, so we willingly comply. In fact, we begin to apply these same procedures to our personal lives. Before we crank up a lawnmower at home, we make an effort to find hearing protection. A genuinely committed organization might demonstrate its authenticity by giving employees written permission to take ear protection and safety glasses home for personal use, furthering its message that safety is now a foundational belief. One organization did this very thing, cementing an expectation of safety well beyond a written rule. By adopting safer practices at home, employees voluntarily and unconsciously raised the bar by assimilating the benefits of hearing and eye protection at home and on the job. In Stage 2, we normalize the policies and procedures from Stage 1 into the context of our daily lives. We make intentional judgment calls about safety. Managers can now focus more on developing and mentoring others for the next step in their safety and professional development.

STAGE 3: INTEGRATE

We move into Stage 3 when we begin to think and behave with others in mind. Safety for ourselves and others has become a core value we choose to nurture and protect. We pay attention to details, such as making sure everyone in the vehicle buckles their seatbelt before we start driving. We understand how to create the lowest risk environment, why it's relevant, and how our behavior can either support or impede safety. We integrate safety into everything we do and recognize the interdependency of crews, teams, and divisions. We understand procurement's role in safety is more than selecting the best value when purchasing equipment; their goal now is to make sure the equipment they choose exceeds the company's safety standards. Seemingly unrelated departments see the value of sharing their work successes and struggles with geographically different sectors to find standardized solutions, and choices and decisions now fall under a broader consideration. Most importantly, employees recognize how their choices affect others, and they make safety a priority.

Other critical factors in developing a No Compromise Safety Culture

SAFETY INFLUENCERS

As discussed previously, one of the most important things you can do for safety— and morale—is to be each other's keeper. When we have a genuine inner desire to help people help themselves, we have become safety influencers. When I first began doing utility work, companies didn't enforce wearing safety glasses like we do today. One of my pole buddies shared a story about how his crewmate chose not to wear them and damaged his vision with welder's burn. This simple story motivated me to wear safety glasses even before they were required. He wasn't my supervisor, a safety professional, or a company leader. His job title was Lineman Journeyman, but his behavior was that of a *safety influencer*. For him, safety was more than simply using instincts to stay out of harm's way, and it was more than understanding safety procedures and policies. This line technician took responsibility for the safety of everyone around him. In Stage 3, people begin to recognize the importance of being a safety influencer.

I've learned over the years that you can't skip a step in the stages of developing a No Compromise Safety Culture. It requires time and diligence. It continuously evolves. Individuals will be at different levels on the journey. We must persistently educate others and gather support. We cannot expect people to be able to integrate something they do not fully understand. To be successful, we must move systematically through the process and reevaluate where we are and where we want to be. Myriad changes such as personnel turnover, new projects, and environmental shifts will affect the process. We must identify these gaps in development and create steps to close them.

CAPTURING HERD SUPPORT WITH CRITICAL MASS

Creating a No Compromise Safety Culture can be daunting. Where do you begin? Ultimately, our goal is to build critical mass—sufficient employee support to achieve self-sustaining results. We need as many people as possible to identify safety as a personal value regardless of their position. There will always be a few detractors who will be a hard sell, but there will always a forward-thinking people who are influencers—supporters who do not need much persuasion to get on board. First, you identify the influencers and maximize their support to help move the potential supporters forward. Once you gain momentum, you'll bring the detractors along as part of the herd.

BELL CURVE MARKETING

I temporarily took a sales position assignment when I worked as an installer/repair technician for the telephone company. During this time, I completed sales training and learned how to apply a bell curve graph to marketing. The bell curve—also called a normal distribution—is the bell-shaped graphic used to show an average distribution of numbers. In academics, teachers use a bell curve to show the distribution of grades. In marketing, people use the bell curve to identify their target audience. If you have a great product presented in a sincere, caring, and honest way, you can capture and persuade up to 80% of a group to buy. It is quite simple to apply this theory to shaping a No Compromise Safety Culture. We know that 20% of the people in our organization will likely support No Compromise with minimal persuasion. Start by identifying these people because they have the highest motivation for safety and the most significant potential to be safety influencers. Next, target the 60% of persuadable people (those in the bell curve) to support the culture change. Once you get 80% of the organization to support a No Compromise Safety Culture, pulling the final 20% into the herd becomes easy. Now you have moved the organization into Stage 3: Integrate.

Safety professionals have many roles.

THE SAFETY CHAMPION

Safety professionals are the champions of safety in the organization. Their primary role is to serve as a resource, advocate, and educator for safety throughout the organization. Although this description sounds simple, the work behind it is not. Safety professionals have responsibility and accountability for safety outcomes.

A SAFETY RESOURCE

As a resource, safety professionals gather, disseminate, and distribute current safety information about state and federal laws and OHSA regulations. They develop and position themselves as experts in safety. If someone pushes back by asking detailed questions about safety methods, they must confidently explain actions, rationale, and decisions using research and methodology appropriate to the audience. For example, you need to be prepared to explain the connection between safety and profits to the CFO. Even though you may have never climbed a utility pole, you need to understand the line technician's job, the mental and physical agility it requires, and communicate your understanding to that person to have credibility.

THE SAFETY ADVOCATE

As advocates, safety professionals lead the organization through the stages of creating a No Compromise Safety Culture. Their top priority is to get as many people as possible to support a No Compromise Safety Culture. Safety advocates identify and recruit influencers who believe in and are enthusiastic about safety. Influencers have progressed to Stage 3 (Integrate) in safety development, can stand pushback, and champion safety for the good of everyone. They understand the benefits of an integrated approach, and they shape their work around developing No Compromise. Safety advocates cultivate the influencers' scope of impact by providing them with continuing education opportunities that help them train others and assume leadership positions in safety. These influencers are the key to moving everyone in the organization through the stages of safety development.

SAFETY EDUCATOR

Safety professionals lead safety education and training. A safety educator's primary mission is to identify where people land in safety development and move them to the next stage with planning, coaching, and training. Do not assume training alone will transform an organization; the safety trainer may be the best OSHA standards safety trainer the company has ever had, but no single skill will develop people to Stage 2.

All of these roles require safety professionals to start with an end goal and a plan. They learn how group dynamics affect human behavior and performance, and they package training and execution into tangible, understandable formats. Safety team members collaborate with frontline leaders to identify gaps and create exercises to address that missing piece of safety. They foster respectful, productive relationships with their peers. Honesty, integrity, professionalism, and open communication are crucial to their success.

If you are a safety champion in your organization, you will probably run into roadblocks. When you have conflict or a disagreement about safety, it's imperative to have an atmosphere of respect where everyone feels comfortable enough to speak up. The more respectful disagreements we have, the more we can accomplish. Pushback makes us think about our methodology and prompts us to figure out why things are not working.

Understand that a No Compromise Safety Culture will not happen in one interaction; it's going to take hundreds of interactions. No Compromise needs to show up in all business areas—in your communications, how you react to challenges, and how you go about your work. Your company's leadership hired you with the expectation that you will make a difference for the organization. They want you to succeed, and they'll help you do so. For them to help you, however, you must make No Compromise part of your core. This attitude will help you withstand any kind of scrutiny that comes your way. Think about what your role *truly* is. As a safety professional, you must have a holistic view of how safety affects the entire organization. You must intelligently articulate the benefits and value a No Compromise Safety Culture brings to each functional area. Your job as a leader in safety is to connect the dots for everyone else to understand your organization's safety goals. This deep understanding helps you give direction to everyone in the organization, from the CEO to the frontline leader to the new employee in the field.

View all incidents as preventable.

As we develop and implement a No Compromise Safety Culture, it's crucial to shift everyone's mindset to view all incidents as preventable. This mindset doesn't mean we jump directly into placing blame after an incident. It means quite the opposite. After an event, we should use hindsight to identify why it happened and what behavior we need to change to prevent a recurrence. We want to be so developed in our culture that we automatically seek knowledge and solutions rather than place blame. Our goal is to find answers to these questions: What are the positives in this? What are the opportunities to improve? What do I need to do to change the outcome next time?

If you're not part of the solution, you're part of the problem.

There are brilliant minds in every organization. Take advantage of the talent around you. Give people the opportunity to challenge, but make sure they provide a possible solution. Theodore Roosevelt supposedly said, "Complaining about a problem without proposing a solution is called whining." If everyone brings a solution to a problem, one is bound to lead to a resolution. In a No Compromise Safety Culture, everyone must own safety and hold each other accountable. Once that starts to happen, the results come. There will undoubtedly be bumps in the road, but the journey is much smoother when we make it easy to move forward.

Develop personal accountability.

When we hear about a person having an incident, it's tempting to think, "Why in the world did this person make that mistake? They must be an idiot." It's an easy way to place blame on someone else instead of accepting personal accountability. It's a Development Stage 1, Learn, response. We see ourselves as disconnected from the event. We miss opportunities to learn and grow, to move into the next stage of development, and to make the change needed to prevent history from repeating itself.

Generally, most incidents result from multiple system breakdowns. One time we had an incident where an employee backed into a stationary object with a company vehicle. They said it wasn't their fault. They claimed the newly installed navigation screen caused them to be distracted. Why did this incident happen? More importantly, why did this person blame someone else? Those of us who operate company equipment and have extensive driver training understand that the driver is responsible for the safe operation of that vehicle. For a No Compromise Safety Culture to work, everyone must have the emotional intelligence and self-awareness to be accountable for safety. Employees should feel comfortable "owning up" to mistakes. Individuals should be held answerable for their actions in a positive way. Company leaders need to recognize that a breakdown in the system may directly result from their leadership. Our goal is to find ways to prevent incidents from happening again through systematic enhancements.

Discourage the normalization of deviance.

Without leadership and personal accountability, incidents may become acceptable results. If you identify a problem but do not address it, you inadvertently create a new standard operating procedure. This normalization of unacceptable behavior gives employees justification to deviate from standardized procedures. They may think, "I do it this way all the time, and nobody ever says anything."

Sometimes, we don't even realize we've deviated from standard procedures. Eventually, this new accepted practice causes everyone to change their perception of specific expectations and acceptable risk in general. In the normalization of deviance, behaviors that were not permitted months or years ago have become the new normal.

Never compromise safety for profit margins.

We are all human and fallible, so we recognize incidents can happen. That's why organizational budgets include funds and insurance to cover the cost of incidents. We want to take care of our people; we should not, however, *plan* for incidents when we plan our jobs. Our planning and bidding should include ways to *prevent* incidents. A manager building in a line item to cover five incidents in a job is akin to a football coach planning to have five fumbles in a game. Like a successful coach, our job should identify how and why these events could happen and plan how to *prevent* them. We always want to win bids and work as efficiently as possible. We cannot, however, compromise safety protocols to gain business and save money.

There is no increase in profits when we compromise safety. Increased risk always equals increased cost. Let's say you're pulling together a plan to set 100 poles. Due to customer demand, you want to get this project completed as quickly as possible. You build your plan with allowances for ten people to have incidents. Will there be a profit? No—not even if the incidents are minor. Instead, strive to create the lowest risk environment by including safety in the planning and bidding process. Invite a safety professional to the pre-bid meeting to help identify potential hazards and plan ways to control them. Set clear expectations about deadlines and safety goals with the customer in advance. Although we can never guarantee zero incidents, we can plan our business around establishing a low-risk work environment while delivering high-quality work.

How to recover from an incident.

Suppose your organization adopts a No Compromise Safety Culture and begins to see improved safety performance. Everyone begins to think and operate with a safety mindset. Creating a low-risk environment becomes standard operating procedure. Morale increases. You celebrate small wins and look for ways to sustain your success.

Then, one day, BAM! You have an incident. Your streak is over. The workers involved feel terrible about breaking the streak; they don't want to be the ones who broke the positive safety performance record. If there is a serious injury or fatality, everyone is disappointed. What should you do next? The Greek philosopher Epictetus said, "It's not what happens to you, but how you react to it that matters."

From a safety perspective, the most important thing you can do after an incident is respond positively and professionally. As you share the news within the organization and answer questions from stakeholders, you must remain calm and professional.

I once worked with an SVP who asked to be informed immediately of all incidents, no matter the time of day or type of event. Whenever I called to report an incident, their reaction was the same. They didn't react negatively, but they didn't downplay the event. They always started by asking about the condition of the employee involved, and they always summarized with, "Thank you for this information. Sounds like you have this handled. Is there anything I may do to help?"

It can be hard to stay positive when we are disappointed. When our attention becomes more focused on incidents, it's easy to react negatively. Interestingly, an incident can become one of the most positive things you have going for you. It can become the event that gives rise to improving seemingly unrelated areas of the organization.

To keep things as positive as possible, consider two important things. First, the people involved didn't deliberately cause it, and second, an incident is not a complete failure. Use it to learn from the past and change course to shape a different future. We love it when our favorite sports team wins big, especially when they do it for several consecutive games or championships. What if your team is losing by a considerable margin at halftime in a championship game? Will the coach try to pump up the team by saying something negative? I doubt it. Great coaches understand the power of positive feedback. They'll enter the locker room with a strategy, ready to talk about what went well in the first half. Then they will explain what went wrong and what the team needs to do to fix it. Championship coaches understand that to change the outcome of a losing game, they need to change their performance. We can do the same thing to change our safety performance. If you are a leader in your organization, your direct reports will look to you for a new strategy. You can focus on the negative and perpetuate a poor performance streak, or you can examine what went wrong and create a plan to fix it. Collaboration is the most effective way to move forward. Your goal should be for everyone to think, "We need to figure out how to prevent this from happening again."

Is it a failure to recognize a hazard or a failure to control a hazard?

There is no such thing as a fluke incident. There is always a root cause. As I look back over my career in safety and in the transmission and distribution industry, I recognize how too much communication happens through the grapevine and gets transferred in many different channels. Since I began working in safety more than thirty years ago, communication norms have evolved. One person used to report a safety situation to a supervisor on a landline phone at the end of the day. Today, thousands of people can view a video on social media before the management team knows an incident has occurred.

Along with this technology, I observed attitudes toward safety incidents shifting. Is safety simply a compliance program that meets the OSHA regulations, or a way of doing business? Now we question whether incidents happen because of a breakdown in communication, or do incidents happen because of behavioral problems? We ask what drives safety in the field and wonder if that is different from what drives safety in the corporate office. Through the evolution of safety as a corporate value, I have learned most incidents fall into two main categories: You either fail to recognize a hazard, or you fail to control the hazard. After that, it becomes pretty straightforward.

Failure to recognize a hazard

Let's say we have a worker who had a minor incident. We might think, "They failed to recognize the hazard. That is a training issue." If a worker doesn't recognize a hazard, it *is* a training issue. Sometimes we aren't training people well enough. Sometimes we promote people too soon, and they become overwhelmed. For the most part, however, experience teaches people how to recognize a hazard. Identifying hazards and understanding the rules and protocols around them falls into Development Stage 1, Learn.

However, few incidents result from a lack of training. What commonly occurs is not a failure to *recognize* a hazard, it is a failure to *control* the hazard. We communicate hazards through job briefings and ongoing safety training. We never deliberately put people in harm's way. It's unlikely we would ask a worker to perform a task without that person understanding all of the potential hazards. The key question is: Was it truly a failure to recognize the hazard, or did they acknowledge the potential for the incident but choose to do the job without *controlling* the hazard to an acceptable level, and why?

Failure to control a hazard

Why would a worker fail to control the hazard? There can be many reasons, including a lack of motivation, guidance, and expectations. We think we can save time, energy, and money by shortcutting accepted practices and procedures. Often failure to control a known hazard results from an employee's attitude. They incorrectly assume the company is just talking big about safety expectations but still valuing the bottom line most. They recognize the hazard exists, but they believe they are too experienced for an incident to happen to them. They may be rushing to wrap up the day. They may simply justify their behavior by thinking, "Just this one time."

Once you figure out the incident resulted from failure to control a hazard, you need to ask: Is this a systemic or an individual problem? Start at the level of the incident and move up the chain of command until you find the weak link. If it's an individual problem, you need to give the person who disregarded the hazard specific training on how and why to control it. If a systemic problem occurs throughout the company, you need to hold a pause appropriate for the magnitude of the situation. You may need to hold a special Monday morning safety meeting or discuss this event at a quarterly meeting. We want to make certain everybody understands how, as an organization, a drift away from a low-risk environment to a high-risk probability is occurring, which potentially leads to a repeat incident somewhere else. Now you need to correct the drift.

Root cause analysis

Root cause analysis is the assessment process used to investigate incidents. It helps us uncover why an incident happened and create a plan to prevent it next time. Root cause analysis begins and ends with a simple, repeated question: "Why?"

Often called the Five Whys, this methodology says we should ask why until we arrive at the root cause. At each step, we consider countermeasures or actions we can take next time to prevent a similar event from recurring. For example, a crew member takes a shortcut, skips wearing gloves and sleeves while performing energized work, and experiences a non-serious electrical incident. The first "why" to ask is: "Why did this person think performing this task without proper PPE was okay?" Maybe the answer is that they've done this task hundreds of times with no problem, so they decided to skip PPE. Then *why* did they think it was okay to flagrantly ignore proper protocols? When seeking a root cause, it's more effective to keep asking "why" and gather short answers. It's necessary to identify step-by-step behavioral actions to prevent an incident from recurring. If we jump to a solution after only a few questions, we may not get to the root cause. A root cause analysis doesn't need to be a formal inquiry that travels to the top of the organization; depending on the severity, many incidents can be investigated and resolved on the local and regional level. It's essential to investigate *all* incidents and near-misses and share the results as learning opportunities. Everyone needs to understand the why of the processes that lead us into Development Stage 2.

Reduce risk by watching for small changes.

Even minor incidents should be acknowledged and communicated. For example, a bee sting may not be as serious as a fall, but it is an incident. What if we downplay the first bee sting, and the next person who gets stung has an allergic reaction and doesn't have an EpiPen? When you examine a series of minor incidents, you should recognize indicators that your level of risk is increasing. Small, incremental changes cause normalization of the unacceptable behavior. We justify our actions because we have developed a habit that seems perfectly normal.

Suppose you start to eat dessert every night after dinner. At first, you don't see much of a change. Then you notice your clothes getting snug. After a few months, you've gained twenty pounds, your pants are too small, your blood sugar is high, and your cholesterol numbers have skyrocketed. Your doctor says you need to start taking medicine and go on a diet and exercise program. You are stunned to hear you can no longer eat dessert! Your small change became a habit that is causing significant problems. We create negative behaviors that lead to poor outcomes when we accept minor incidents and incremental changes that deviate from acceptable practice. More importantly, we allow our casual attitude about safety protocols to transform our culture negatively. Many organizations refer to these new behaviors as drift. To prevent drift from developing into more serious incidents, they implement a Drift Audit Assessment that pinpoints deviations from regularly accepted safety practices *before* they become a serious issue.

Build momentum.

Development Stage 3, Integrate, is where we really start to gain momentum. Safety permeates every area of the organization. Everyone appreciates how their work affects safety outcomes. Employees take ownership and pride in the organization's positive safety record and maximize the benefits of these safety achievements by measuring and sharing outcomes, repeating success stories, and publicly praising the people involved. Genuinely honest appreciation for accomplishment means a lot to people; use positive communication to boost morale, increase adaptation, and sustain long-lasting behaviors.

Consider how human behavior and company leadership impact safety. Most highly successful people work for managers who lead with constructive feedback through ongoing, positive reinforcement. People make mistakes, but they usually adopt new behaviors that reduce the risk of recurrence when they understand how and why mistakes happen. Effective managers understand the value behind servant leadership and respect human performance. They don't demand perfection, but they do expect excellence and an attitude of continuous improvement.

Never let the spinning plates fall.

If you were born after 1971, you might never have seen the *Ed Sullivan Show*, but you may have heard how the show hosted the Beatles' first performance in America. You also may have heard people say they have "too many spinning plates" when they feel overwhelmed with tasks. The *Ed Sullivan Show* can take credit for both things: the Beatles sharing rock 'n roll with America and Erich Brenn spinning plates on the tops of wooden sticks.

Both were guests of the show. When I was a kid, my family would go to church on Sunday night, and then we'd hurry home to watch the *Ed Sullivan Show*, on which Brenn was a frequent guest. I always marveled at his ability to keep eight plates and four bowls spinning on top of long wooden poles at once. He ran around the table, twisting the wooden poles to spin the plates and bowls and keep them balanced. As long as the plates and bowls were moving, nothing would fall. When I thought about this act from a safety perspective, it reminded me of how we often hear people in our industry talk about the many tasks they need to complete. "I need to finish that report." "I need to get back to my manager with the answer to that question." "I need to fix this problem *now*." What they're actually saying is that they have a lot of plates to spin. The idea behind a No Compromise Safety Culture is that everyone grabs a wooden pole and twists it. Suddenly, it isn't so hard to keep all those plates spinning. If we keep everybody engaged, involved, and trained, creating a No Compromise Safety Culture and sustaining the momentum becomes much easier.

Sustaining momentum

As we integrated a No Compromise Safety Culture in one of my organizations, we began to see excellent results. We started our No Compromise journey with fifteen people talking about safety in a company conference room. Within ten years, we grew to 1,100 people attending a safety summit at the local Expo Center. Our CEO and top leaders presented. We heard from contract leadership. We even had a regulatory leader talk about our partnership between organizations. Our recordable injury rate dropped to a record low, and we won safety awards. Everyone accepted responsibility for their own safety and the safety of others. We had integrated safety throughout the organization, and we began a period of sustained momentum.

You cannot put safety on autopilot.

An ongoing challenge to the No Compromise Culture of Safety is keeping the momentum going. It's easy to shift into autopilot. Suppose three people form a crew that has worked together for a year. At first, as they get to know each other, they communicate more frequently. They set up safety zones with pre-job communication. They use open and three-way communication to go about tasks safely. After a while, they talk less and less as they work. They may not realize they've stopped communicating. They've done this work together so many times, they've shifted into autopilot.

Now there's a higher probability this established crew will drift from safety. They are more likely to fall into the normalization of deviance. Avoid normalization of deviance with ongoing organizational enhancements. Be creative as you identify ways to keep everyone engaged. Establish a safety council with your safety influencers. Create safety committees within each division. Alternate areas of responsibility. Put people with fresh eyes on a different team to help you identify drift. If one idea doesn't work, scrap it, and try something else. The kind of enhancement you use is less important than the result you get.

Strike a balance with success.

After our organization began to sustain momentum, we beat our original year-end safety goal of a 1.5 recordable rate halfway through the year with a 1.2. Everyone was ecstatic until the number crept up to 1.3. They started worrying about upward trends, and everyone began talking about our safety success negatively. While everyone was wringing their hands and looking for the sky to fall, *we remained well below our original goal*. We didn't need to worry about the sky falling because we had a contingency plan for that.

As a No Compromise Safety Culture becomes more integrated and we achieve our safety goals, our standard of excellence increases. We expect more because continuous improvement is now part of our DNA. The desired optimum outcome will always be zero incidents. An unintended consequence of success is that we sometimes let the numbers manage us. Continuous improvement may not change the recordable number of injuries, but understanding success at the end game is different from setting goals between stages one, two, and three. How we react to success can influence future outcomes. We do not want to unintentionally communicate that we don't appreciate each person's commitment to safety or that we are content with the status quo.

Many factors influence safety across industries, and work environments never stop changing. We must adapt continually to new technology, higher standards, and changes in the workplace. In success, it becomes more critical we set smart, attainable goals. What worked perfectly yesterday may not work today.

Be careful not to let your numbers dictate your success. Don't let goal setting conflict with the success that got you there. Use metrics as a tool. Find the balance of acceptable metrics and realistic goals. Determine your safety program's point of diminishing returns—that point where extra effort no longer improves outcome. Your goal may evolve to safety maintenance rather than incident reduction or change mid-year due to unforeseen circumstances. Continuous improvement can stretch goals to achieve a certain point. However, we cannot be so engrossed in continuous improvement that we misidentify the success of our safety program. Our end game in safety is different from anywhere else. In many ways, it's harder to sustain an excellent safety record than it is to attain one. The true measure of a safety culture is more than metrics, it is our authentic safety culture demonstrated by what employees do when nobody is watching.

Summary of Safety Truth #9: Safety is not just about you.

The only way to create and sustain a positive safety performance is to see it as a team effort. It's not just the responsibility of the safety department. The *entire* organization must integrate safety goals into their respective divisions. If you take your time and focus on the positive results, you'll begin a cultural shift, no matter how small. In a No Compromise Safety Culture, everyone embraces safety all the time. We celebrate successes, share failures, and find ways to prevent recurrence as a team. We carry everyone through the three stages of development. As our integrated safety culture strengthens, risk reduces. Small wins lead to big wins. We build momentum by learning ways to better understand, identify, and remove risk, and we tenaciously and relentlessly deploy that learning to make the next day. With a No Compromise Safety Culture, we never guarantee zero incidents, but we can guarantee a lower risk environment for everyone.

About the Author

With forty-three years of experience in the utilities industry, Ken Sheridan is recognized as a key influencing factor in making Louisville Gas and Electric and Kentucky Utilities (LG&E and KU) companies and Davis H. Elliot Company, Inc. among the top utility industry safety performers nationally and internationally.

Sheridan's aggressive and energetic approach to safety, combined with the implementation of behavior-based techniques, is the key to his positive impact on employees and business partners. As a result of his influence, LG&E and KU won many national and international awards and frequently serves as a benchmark for other companies' safety goals. Ken was instrumental in enhancing safety awareness and performance among utilities and organizations in the U.S. and abroad, including the United Kingdom and Albania. Ken served as Director of Safety and Technical Training, Director of Operations and Public Safety, Operations Manager, District Manager, Service Manager, and Safety Coordinator.

Nearly five years ago, Ken joined the Davis H. Elliot Company, where he created and developed the No Compromise Moments video library and served on the SIF Prevention Team. To this day, he remains a member of the Davis H. Elliot Corporate Safety Governance Team. While working for Davis H. Elliot, Ken wrote and published his first book, *No Compromise: The Truth about Workplace Safety & Business Success*.

In addition, Ken served as chair of the Kentucky Labor Cabinet's Apprenticeship and Training Council since 2006, a position for which he was appointed by the Kentucky governor. He graduated from Murray State University in 1973 with a bachelor's degree in health and sociology and completed numerous hours of postgraduate work in the field of human relations.

Made in the USA
Middletown, DE
28 July 2022

70139937R10071